Mises on Money

Mises on Money

Gary North

Ludwig von Mises Institute
518 West Magnolia Avenue
Auburn, Alabama 36832
mises.org

ISBN: 978-1-61016-248-7

This book is dedicated to

Tom Woods
an historian who has crossed
over into economics, and to

Tom DiLorenzo
an economist who has crossed
over into history, and to

David Gordon
a philosopher who has crossed
over into history and economics.

TABLE OF CONTENTS

Introduction 9

1. Money: A Market-Generated Phenomenon 15

2. The Optimum Quantity of Money 33

3. Two Myths: Neutral Money and Stable Prices 55

4. Fractional Reserve Banking 71

5. The Monetary Theory of the Business Cycle 99

Conclusion 115

Index 141

INTRODUCTION

Ludwig von Mises (1881–1973) made a major contribution to the theory of money with the publication of his book, *The Theory of Money and Credit* (1912). He was 31 years old. It was translated into English in 1924. It was updated in 1934. The 1934 edition was reprinted, without changes except for an appendix, in 1953 by Yale University Press. It had previously been published in England.

He followed this path-breaking book with what has proven to be one of the most important essays in the history of economic theory: "Economic Calculation in the Socialist Commonwealth" (1920). In it, he argued that without capital markets based on private ownership, socialist central planners are economically blind. They cannot know either the economic value or the price of capital goods. Therefore, they cannot know which resources should be allocated to meet the desires of consumers, including the State itself. He expanded this essay into a book, *Socialism: An Economic and Sociological Analysis* (1922). A second German edition appeared in 1932, the year before Hitler became Chancellor of Germany. This was the edition used to translate the English-language edition, published in 1951 by Yale University Press. Mises added an Epilogue, which began with these words: "Nothing is more unpopular today than the free market economy, i.e., capitalism." It ended with these words: "Not mythical 'material productive forces,' but reason and ideas determine the course of human affairs. What is needed to stop the trend towards socialism and despotism is common sense and moral courage."

More than any other economist, it was Mises who offered the most detailed theoretical critique of socialism. But, as it turned out, it was not sound ideas, but the economic irrationality of socialist economic planning that finally undermined the envy-driven, power-loving, statist religion of socialism. Socialism by 1989 had bankrupted its most powerful incarnation, the Soviet Union. When it fell in 1991, socialist economists found themselves with few followers. Overnight, socialism had become a joke. Books on "what Marx really meant" filled the "books for a buck" bins in college-town bookstores. Socialist professors never had a plausible economic theory; they had only tenure. As the pro-socialist and millionaire economics textbook author Robert Heilbroner finally admitted in *The New Yorker* in 1990, "Mises was right." Heilbroner's ideological academic peers have not been equally honest over the last two decades.

Mises's last major book was *Human Action: A Treatise on Economics* (Yale University Press, 1949). *Human Action* presented a comprehensive theory of the free market on the one hand and an equally comprehensive critique of economic interventionism by civil government on the other.

The timing of the publication of *Human Action* could not have been worse. It was the year after the publication of Paul Samuelson's textbook, *Economics*, which went on to sell four million copies and shape economics students' thinking without significant opposition for almost two decades. It is still in print. By 1949, the Keynesian revolution was in full operation in American classrooms outside of the University of Chicago. In contrast, Mises was a little-known Austrian immigrant whose major theoretical contributions to economics were long forgotten, relics of an ante-bellum, pre-Keynesian world. He was teaching in an academically peripheral university that did not even bother to pay him out of its own funds. His salary was paid by a handful of supporters, most notably Lawrence Fertig. There Mises taught his graduate seminars until 1969, when he retired at age 88. He died in 1973, making him ineligible for the Nobel Prize in economic science. The next year, his former disciple, F. A. Hayek, shared the Nobel Prize with socialist Gunnar Myrdal. (It was said at the time that Hayek never expected to win it, and Myrdal never expected to share it.) Hayek won in part on the basis of his theory of the business cycle, developed in the 1930s, which was based almost entirely on Mises's *Theory of Money and Credit*, and also for his theory of the free market as a transmitter of accurate information, a theory developed originally by Mises in *Socialism*, which had converted Hayek from his youthful socialist leanings, as he later said publicly. But Hayek had used a few charts in the 1930s. Mises never did. Hayek was clearly scientific; Mises clearly wasn't. Thus is academic performance rewarded by the economics profession.

In the war of ideas against monetary debasement and then socialism, Mises served as the lone Marine who led the initial assaults against the statists' machine gun nests in academia. He did it from outside academia's walls. The University of Vienna never hired its most distinguished economics graduate. Hayek was part of the third wave: Mises's early disciples, who began volunteering for duty in the early 1920s. These included Lionel Robbins, Wilhelm Röpke, and several world-famous economists who by 1940 had left "military service" to become part of the "diplomatic corps," seeking a cease-fire with the enemy. For this, they were rewarded well by the enemy: major publishing houses, academic tenure, and the honorary presidency of at least one regional economics association. Yet at age 88, Mises was still tossing grenades at the enemy's bunkers. (Hayek also remained on duty in the field, but he was always more of a sniper.)

In summarizing Mises's theory of money, I draw heavily on his two major works that dealt with monetary theory, *The Theory of Money and Credit* and *Human Action*, plus a few minor books. I cover five themes: the definition of money; the optimum quantity of money, and how to achieve it; the myth of neutral money and its corollary, stable prices; fractional reserve banking, and how to inhibit it; and the monetary theory of the business cycle. They are closely interrelated. Mises's system was a system.

I wrote this book in five days in late January 2002. I did so in response to Jude Wanniski's decision to publish an e-mail exchange I had with him on the gold standard.[1] He led off with this:

> Both North and Rockwell have been disagreeing with my contention that the U.S. has been in the grip of a monetary deflation for the past five years, insisting a deflation does not occur until price indices are in negative territory. And like the monetarists, they point out that the monetary aggregates have been growing, which to them is a sign of inflation, not deflation.

As of early 2012, consumer prices are up 26 percent since 2002.[2] In short, Wanniski was as bad in predicting price deflation as he was in defending the case for gold.

I was always convinced that Wanniski did not understand Mises, Austrian School economics, or the traditional gold standard, yet he repeatedly claimed Mises as an early supply-side economist. Mises was no supply-side economist. Wanniski's decision to publish our exchange finally pushed me over the edge. When I go over the edge, I usually write something. *Mises on Money* was the result.

Wanniski refused to respond in print. He had a staffer write a response.[3] The staffer tried to argue, as Wanniski had argued, that modern Austrian School economists, especially those in

---

[1] "Exchange With an Austrian" (Jan. 2, 2002). (http://bit.ly/NorthWanniski)

[2] Inflation calculator, Bureau of Labor Statistics. (http://bit.ly/BLScalc)

[3] Nathan Lewis, "The Austrian School and the 'Austrian' School." (http://bit.ly/LewisOnMises)

the Rothbard tradition, are not "true" Austrian School economists, and that the supply-siders are the true heirs—a contention that no other supply-side economist previously argued. They knew better. Gene Callahan responded to this response a few days later. His response was posted on LewRockwell.com on January 31. (http://bit.ly/gcgnlewis)

I

MONEY: A MARKET-GENERATED PHENOMENON

Mises began his presentation in Part I, Chapter I of *The Theory of Money and Credit* with a discussion of voluntary exchange. In a society without exchange, money is unnecessary. Mises said specifically in the book's first paragraph that money is also not needed in theory in a pure socialist commonwealth (p. 29). By contrast, in a private property order, "The function of money is to facilitate the business of the market by acting as a common medium of exchange" (p. 29).

Direct exchange is barter. Barter is associated with a low division of labor. Participants expect to consume whatever it is that they receive in exchange. But in a more developed system of indirect exchange, participants exchange their goods and services for goods that can be exchanged for additional goods and services. Mises then explained why certain commodities become the widely accepted means of exchange, i.e., money. He distinguished between two kinds of goods. This conceptual distinction is fundamental to his theory of money.

> Now all goods are not equally marketable. While there is only a limited and occasional demand for certain goods, that for others is more general and constant. Consequently, those who bring goods of the first kind to market in order to exchange them for goods that they

> need themselves have as a rule a smaller prospect of success than those who offer goods of the second kind. If, however, they exchange their relatively unmarketable goods for such as are more marketable, they will get a step nearer to their goal and may hope to reach it more surely and economically than if they had restricted themselves to direct exchange. It was in this way that those goods that were originally the most marketable became common media of exchange; that is, goods into which all sellers of other goods first converted their wares and which it paid every would-be buyer of any other commodity to acquire first. And as soon as those commodities that were relatively most marketable had become common media of exchange, there was an increase in the difference between their marketability and that of all other commodities, and this in its turn further strengthened and broadened their position as media of exchange (p. 32). . . .
>
> This stage of development in the use of media of exchange, the exclusive employment of a single economic good, is not yet completely attained. In quite early times, sooner in some places than in others, the extension of indirect exchange led to the employment of the two precious metals gold and silver as common media of exchange. But then there was a long interruption in the steady contraction of the group of goods employed for that purpose. For hundreds, even thousands, of years the choice of mankind has wavered undecided between gold and silver (p. 33).

Mises made his point unmistakably clear: "It was in this way that those goods that were originally the most marketable became common media of exchange." Mises therefore defined money as the most marketable commodity. "It is the most marketable good which people accept because they want to offer it in later acts of impersonal exchange" (*Human Action*, p. 398).

Money facilitates credit transactions. What are credit transactions? "Credit transactions are in fact nothing but the exchange of present goods against future goods" (*TM&C*, p. 35).

We now have Mises's definitions of money (the most marketable commodity) and credit (the exchange of present goods for hoped-for future goods).

Money serves as a transmitter of value through time because certain goods serve as media of exchange. Why do they so serve? Because of "the special suitability of goods for hoarding" (p. 35). This economic function of money also involves the transport of value through space. It is not that money circulates that makes it money. Lots of goods circulate. It is that money is hoarded—is in someone's possession as a cash balance—that is crucial for its service as a medium of exchange. He wrote that "it must be recognized that from the economic point of view there is no such thing as money lying idle" (p. 147). In other words, "all money must be regarded at rest in the cash reserve of some individual or other."

> What is called storing money is a way of using wealth. The uncertainty of the future makes it seem advisable to hold a larger or smaller part of one's possessions in a form that will facilitate a change from one way of using wealth to another, or transition from the ownership of one good to that of another, in order to preserve the opportunity of being able without difficulty to satisfy urgent demands that may possibly arise in the future for goods that will have to be obtained by exchange (p. 147).

Because we live in ignorance about an uncertain future, we hold money: the most marketable commodity. Because it is highly marketable, it provides us with the most options, no matter what happens. If we had better knowledge of the future, we would hold whatever good is most likely to be most in demand in the new conditions, in order to maximize our profits. But we do not know, so we settle for holding money. We gain a lower rate of profit, but we gain much greater security in preserving exchange value.

MONEY IS NOT A MEASURE OF VALUE

Money transmits value, Mises taught, but money does not measure value. This distinction is fundamental in Mises's theory of money. "Money is neither an abstract *numéraire* nor a standard of value or prices. It is necessarily an economic good and as such it is valued and appraised on its own merits, i.e., the services which a man expects from holding cash. On the market there is [sic] always change and movement. Only because there are fluctuations is there money" (*Human Action*, pp. 414–15).

Any economic theory that teaches that money measures economic value, or that any civil government should establish policies that preserve the value of money because money is a measure of value, is anti-Misesian. You must understand this conclusion if the remainder of this study is to make any sense at all. *The call for government-induced stable purchasing power, with or without a government-licensed monopolistic central bank, is an anti-Misesian call for government intervention into the economy.* Mises was opposed to government intervention into the economy, including the monetary system.

Mises was adamant: *there is no measure of economic value.* He was a disciple of Carl Menger. Menger was a proponent of a strictly subjective theory of economic value. Mises insisted that there is no objective way to measure subjective value. He began Chapter 2, "On the Measurement of Value," with these words: "Although it is usual to speak of money as a measure of value and prices, the notion is entirely fallacious. So long as the subjective theory of value is accepted, this question of measurement cannot arise" (*TM&C*, p. 38). Subjective valuation "arranges commodities in order of their significance; it does not measure its significance" (p. 39). It ranks significance; it does not measure it. This is the theme of Chapter 2.

> If it is impossible to measure subjective use-value, it follows directly that it is impracticable to ascribe "quantity" to it. We may say, the value of this commodity is greater than the value of that; but it is not permissible for us to assert, this commodity is worth *so much*. Such a way of speaking necessarily implies a definite unit. It really amounts to stating how many times a given unit is contained in the quantity to be defined. But this kind of calculation is quite inapplicable to processes of valuation (p. 45).

The fact that money does not measure value is a crucially important aspect of Mises's theory of money. Perhaps this analogy will help clarify his reasoning.

DO YOU LOVE ME?

A wife asks: "Do you love me?" Her husband dutifully answers: "Of course I do." She presses the issue: "How much do you love me?" He answers: "A lot." She continues: "Do you love me more than you used to love your ex-girlfriend?" He replies: "Yes, I do." So far, we are still in the realm of subjective value.

She presses the issue. "You used to be wild about her. I remember. You don't act very wild about me. Do you love me more now than you loved her back then?" This raises the question of the permanence of value scales over time. The problem is, these scales of value change. Also, we forget what they were, and how intensely they registered with us. A truth-telling husband may reply: "I just don't remember." Or he may say, "I love you more now than I loved her back then," mentally defining "love" to make the statement true. But how can he be sure what he felt back then? His memory has faded, along with his passion. This is the philosophical problem of subjective valuation through time. No one on earth possesses a permanent subjective value scale that measures changes in one's temporal subjective value scale.

Next, she moves to objective value. "Exactly how much more do you love me than you used to love her?" Now he faces a dilemma, both personal and epistemological. She has moved from a consideration of his subjective scale of values to an objective measure of subjective value. Here is his epistemological dilemma: there is no objective measure of subjective value. A subjective value scale is *ordinal*—first, second, third—rather than *cardinal*, i.e., "exactly this much more." Subjective values are ranked, not measured.

A wise husband with a knowledge of the Bible might try to end the discussion by saying, "I love you more than rubies." Solomon said something like this. "Who can find a virtuous woman for her price is far above rubies?" (Proverbs 31:10). But even Solomon did not say exactly how much above rubies her price is.

There is no objective measure of subjective values. A diamond may be forever; it does not measure subjective value. Nothing on earth does.

COMPARE, YES; MEASURE, NO

Mises said that every economic act involves a comparison of values (*TM&C*, p. 38). A person chooses among several commodities (p. 38). He exchanges one commodity for another. "For this reason it has been said that every economic act may be regarded as a kind of exchange" (p. 39). Mises in *Human Action* made central this idea of human action as exchange: an exchange of conditions. "Action is an attempt to substitute a more satisfactory state of affairs for a less satisfactory one. We call such a willfully induced alteration an exchange. A less desirable condition is bartered for a more desirable." (*Human Action*, Chapter IV, Sect. 4: "Action as an Exchange.")

Nevertheless, the exchange is not based on someone's measure of value, merely his comparison of value: more vs. less. As he said, "The judgement, 'Commodity *a* is worth more to me than commodity *b*' no more presupposes a measure of economic value than the judgement (A is dearer to me—more highly esteemed—than B) presupposes a measure of friendship" (*TM&C*, pp. 44–45). This means that "There is no such thing as abstract value" (p. 47). There are only specific acts of valuation. Money does measure objective prices (ratios of exchange). "If in this sense we wish to attribute to money the function of being a measure of prices, there is no reason why we should not do so" (p. 49). Admitting that money measures objective prices is not the same as saying that money is a measure of value, which is subjective. Money does not measure value. Mises was quite clear: "What has been said should have made sufficiently plain the unscientific nature of the practice of attributing to money the function of acting as a measure of price or even of value. Subjective value is not measured, but graded. The problem of the measurement of objective use-value is not an economic problem at all" (p. 47).

I emphasize this because we hear, over and over, such phrases as this:

> There is nothing more important that the government can provide individual producers than a reliable standard of value, a unit of account that retains its constancy as a measuring device.

This statement is completely contrary to Mises's theory of *subjective economic value*, on which his theory of money rests. It is contrary to Mises's theory of civil government. It is contrary to the concept of *free market money*, as Mises described it. In short, it is contrary to Misesian economics. Forewarned is forearmed.

FOUR KINDS OF MONEY

Mises said that there are four kinds of money: token (base metal) coins, commodity money, credit money, and fiat money (pp. 59–62). Commodity money is what the free market has determined is the most marketable commodity, and therefore the medium of exchange. It is "a commercial commodity."

> We may give the name *commodity money* to that sort of money that is at the same time a commercial commodity; and the name *fiat money* to money that comprises things with a special legal qualification. A third category may be called *credit money*, this being that sort of money which constitutes a claim against any physical or legal person. But these claims must not be both payable on demand and absolutely secure; if they were, there could be no difference between their value and that of the sum of money to which they referred, and they could not be subjected to an independent process of valuation on the part of those who dealt with them. In some way or other the maturity of these claims must be postponed to some future time (p. 61).

Mises's definition of credit money distinguishes credit money from a receipt for money. Credit money is not "both payable on demand and absolutely secure." It is not the same as that which we can call warehouse receipts for commodity money, in which case "there could be no difference between their value and that of the sum of money to which they referred." In *Human Action*, he defined a warehouse receipt for money metal coins a money-certificate. "If the debtor—the government or a bank—keeps against the whole amount of money-substitutes a 100 percent reserve of money proper, we call the money-substitute a *money-certificate*" (p. 430). A money-certificate is both payable on demand and secure. It is not a promise to pay at some date in the future. It is a promise to pay immediately on demand, a promise that can be fulfilled in all cases because there is money metal on reserve to meet all of the receipts even if they were presented for redemption on the same day. Money-certificates function as money because they are the equivalent of the commodity money that they represent. For each money-certificate issued, the equivalent weight of coins is withdrawn from circulation. "Changes in the quantity of money-certificates therefore do not alter the supply of money and the money relation. They do not play any role in the determination of the purchasing power of money" (p. 430).

Credit money is money that has less than a 100 percent reserve in coins. "If the money reserve kept by the debtor against the money-substitute issued is less than the total amount of such substitutes, we call the amount of substitutes which exceeds the reserve *fiduciary media*. As a rule it is not possible to ascertain whether a concrete specimen of money-substitutes is a money-certificate or a fiduciary medium." Fiduciary media increase the amount of money in circulation. "The issue of fiduciary media enlarges the bank's funds available for lending beyond these limits" (p. 430).

Money is a commodity, Mises insisted. It is not a promise to pay. Fiduciary media is a promise to pay. It is a promise that cannot be fulfilled at the same time to everyone who has been issued fiduciary media.

The value of a coin is based on the weight and fineness of its metal.

> Nevertheless, in defiance of all official regulations and prohibitions and fixing of prices and threats of punishment, commercial practice has always insisted that what has to be considered in valuing coins is not their face value but their value as metal. The value of a coin has always been determined, not by the image and superscription it bears nor by the proclamation of the mint and market authorities, but by its metal content (*TM&C*, p. 65).

FREE COINAGE, NOT STATE MONOPOLY

Civil governments in the past have issued coins or ingots with a stamp on them that certifies their weight and fineness. In the short run, at least, this was a benefit to market participants:

it reduced their search costs for reliable coinage. "But in the hands of liberal governments the character of this state monopoly was completely altered. The ideas which considered it an instrument of interventionist policies were discarded. No longer was it used for fiscal purposes or for favoring some groups of the people at the expense of other groups" (*Human Action*, p. 776). But, he goes on to say, "On the other hand, individuals were entitled to bring bullion to the mint and to have it transformed into standard coins either free of charge or against payments of a seigniorage [fee] generally not surpassing the actual "expenses of the process" (p. 776).

Stamping coins is not part of the provision of civil justice, which alone justifies a State monopoly, according to his utilitarian democratic political theory (p. 149). This is the only case I know in all of Mises's writings where he identified as beneficial to society a zero-fee, monopolistic service offered by civil government to citizens, despite the fact that stamping coins is not part of what he regarded as civil government's legitimate monopoly of law enforcement by violence. He did not say that he recommended this practice. He said only that liberal governments for a time did not abuse their declared monopoly over coin stamping.

In Mises's theory of money, money is not what the State says it is—what he called the "nominalist" theory of money. Money is what the free market says it is: the most marketable commodity. He ended Chapter 3 of *Theory of Money and Credit* with a call for free coinage: a denial of the State's monopoly over money. He rejected nominalism and affirmed free coinage. Nominalism leads to the State's establishment of its own monopolistic money substitutes, which State officials insist are money, but which are of less value, according to the free market's assessment.

> The nominalists assert that the monetary unit, in modern countries at any rate, is not a concrete

commodity unit that can be defined in suitable technical terms, but a nominal quantity of value about which nothing can be said except that it is created by law. Without touching upon the vague and nebulous nature of this phraseology, which will not sustain a moment's criticism from the point of view of the theory of value, let us simply ask: *What, then, were the mark, the franc, and the pound before 1914?* Obviously, they were nothing but certain weights of gold. Is it not mere quibbling to assert that Germany had not a gold standard but a mark standard? According to the letter of the law, Germany was on a gold standard, and the mark was simply the unit of account, the designation of 1/2790 kg. of refined gold. This is in no way affected by the fact that nobody was bound in private dealings to accept gold ingots or foreign gold coins, for the whole aim and intent of State intervention in the monetary sphere is simply to release individuals from the necessity of testing the weight and fineness of the gold they receive, a task which can only be undertaken by experts and which involves very elaborate precautionary measures. The narrowness of the limits within which the weight and fineness of the coins are legally allowed to vary at the time of minting, and the establishment of a further limit to the permissible loss by wear of those in circulation, are much better means of securing the integrity of the coinage than the use of scales and nitric acid on the part of all who have commercial dealings. Again, the right of free coinage, one of the basic principles of modern monetary law, is a protection in the opposite direction against the emergence of a difference in value between the coined and uncoined metal (pp. 66–67). . . .

The role played by ingots in the gold reserves of the banks is a proof that the monetary standard consists in the precious metal, and not in the proclamation of the authorities (p. 67).

In Chapter 4, "Money and the State," Mises made clear that the State does not establish economic laws of exchange. It is subordinate to these laws. Mises even capitalized this phrase: Laws of Price.

> The position of the State in the market differs in no way from that of any other parties to commercial transactions. Like these others, the State exchanges commodities and money on terms which are governed by the Laws of Price. It exercises its sovereign rights over its subjects to levy compulsory contributions from them; but in all other respects it adapts itself like everybody else to the commercial organization of society. As a buyer or seller the State has to conform to the conditions of the market. If it wishes to alter any of the exchange ratios established in the market, it can only do this through the market's own mechanism. As a rule it will be able to act more effectively than anyone else, thanks to the resources at its command outside the market (p. 68). . . .
>
> The concept of money as a creature of Law and the State is clearly untenable. It is not justified by a single phenomenon of the market. To ascribe to the State the power of dictating the laws of exchange, is to ignore the fundamental principles of money-using society (p. 69).

The State passes laws and enforces them, but this does not change the laws of value. It merely produces results that are in conformity to the laws of value. For example, consider the free market's establishment of two forms of money, gold and silver coins. The State stamps metal coins as being of a particular weight and fineness. The specified weight and fineness are not specified on each coin, but by law, the coins must meet a specified standard. Mises called this coinage system a "parallel standard." The free market establishes their value based on the value of their metals. "This stage was reached without further State influence" (p. 72).

At some point, the State intervenes by establishing a legal exchange rate between the parallel systems of coinage, despite the fact that for thousands of years the systems have flourished in the free market (p. 75). As soon as the free market's price for each metal deviates from the State's legal parity—a system of price controls—Gresham's law takes over. This was the observation by Queen Elizabeth's royal factor in Antwerp, Sir Thomas Gresham, that "bad money drives out good money." Mises clarified Gresham's law in *Human Action*. "It would be more correct to say that the money which the government's decree has undervalued disappears from the market and the money which the decree has overvalued remains" (p. 447). Consumers hoard the undervalued coins, or use them in illegal black market exchanges at ratios that deviate from the law's fixed ratios, or send them abroad, where the coins purchase goods of equal market value. People then spend the overvalued coins in public.

The result of this government price-setting is always a monometallic standard in the legal markets of the nation: either gold or silver. This is the free market's response to price controls on the two metals. This result may not have been the policy-makers' intention.

> The primary result of this was a decision, for a little while at least, between the two precious metals. Not that this was what the state had intended. On the contrary, the State had no thought whatever of deciding in favor of the use of one or the other metal; it had hoped to secure the circulation of both. But the official regulation, which in declaring the reciprocal substitutability of gold and silver money overestimated the market ratio of the one in terms of the other, merely succeeded in differentiating the utility of the two for monetary purposes. The consequence was the increased employment of one of the metals and the disappearance of the other. The legislative and judicial intervention of the state had

> completely failed. It had been demonstrated, in striking fashion, that the state alone could not make a commodity into a common medium of exchange, that is, into money, but that this could be done only by the common action of all the individuals engaged in business (pp. 75–76).
>
> But what the State fails to achieve through legislative means may be to a certain degree within its power as controller of the mint. It was in the latter capacity that the State intervened when the alternative standard was replaced by permanent monometallism. This happened in various ways. The transition was quite simple and easy when the action of the State consisted in preventing a return to the temporarily undervalued metal in one of the alternating monometallic periods by rescinding the right of free coinage. The matter was even simpler in those countries where one or the other metal had gained the upper hand before the State had reached the stage necessary for the modern type of regulation, so that all that remained for the law to do was to sanction a situation that was already established (p. 76).

In other cases, the transition was deliberate. But the free market's laws of price always governed the transition. This was especially true of the State's attempted establishment of economic parity between credit money and money metal coinage. Gresham's law still rules.

> The exaggeration of the importance in monetary policy of the power at the disposal of the State in its legislative capacity can only be attributed to superficial observation of the processes involved in the transition from commodity money to credit money. This transition has normally been achieved by means of a state declaration that inconvertible claims to money were as good means of payment as money itself. As a rule, it has not been the object of such a declaration to carry out a change of standard and substitute credit money for commodity money. In the great majority of cases, the

> state has taken such measures merely with certain fiscal ends in view. It has aimed to increase its own resources by the creation of credit money. In the pursuit of such a plan as this, the diminution of the money's purchasing power could hardly seem desirable. And yet it has always been this depreciation in value which, through the coming into play of Gresham's law, has caused the change of monetary standard. It would be quite out of harmony with the facts to assert that cash payments had ever been stopped; that is, that the permanent convertability of the notes had been suspended, with the intention of effecting a transition to a credit standard. This result has always come to pass against the will of the State, not in accordance with it (p. 77).

In order to affect the acceptance of fiat money or credit money, the State adopts a policy of the abolition of its previous contractual obligations. What was previously a legal right of full convertability into either gold or silver coins is abolished by a new law. The State removes the individual's legal right to exchange the State's paper notes for gold or silver coins. It then declares that the new, inconvertible fiat paper money or bank credit money is equal in value to the older redeemable notes, meaning equal to the value of the actual coins previously obtainable through redemption. But the free market determines otherwise. The two forms of money are not equal in value in the judgment of the market's individual participants. Gresham's law is still obeyed.

> Business usage alone can transform a commodity into a common medium of exchange. It is not the State, but the common practice of all those who have dealings in the market, that creates money. It follows that state regulation attributing general power of debt liquidation to a commodity is unable of itself to make that commodity into money. If the State creates credit money—and this is naturally true in a still greater degree of fiat money—it can do so only by taking things that

> are already in circulation as money substitutes (that is, as perfectly secure and immediately convertible claims to money) and isolating them for purposes of valuation by depriving them of their essential characteristic of permanent convertability. Commerce would always protect itself against any other method of introducing a government credit currency. The attempt to put credit money into circulation has never been successful, except when the coins or notes in question have already been in circulation as money substitutes (pp. 77–78).

CONCLUSION

According to Mises, money is the most marketable commodity. Historically, money has been gold and silver. Money-certificates are receipts for money metals that are backed 100 percent by these metals. They function as money because they are exchangeable for specified quantities of money metal at any time without restriction. There are three other kinds of money: credit money (money-certificates that are not 100 percent backed by money metals), low-denomination token coins made of base metals, and fiat money (certificates designated by the State as money, but not backed by anything—no promise to pay anything).

The State can set legal prices, meaning exchange ratios, between the various kinds of money. The effects of such fixed exchange rates are identical to the effects of any other kind of price control: gluts and shortages. The artificially overvalued money (glut) replaces the artificially undervalued money (shortage). This cause-and-effect relationship is called Gresham's law.

The free market establishes free coinage. The State in the past has stamped certain coins or ingots with its identifying mark, as a means of validating the weight and fineness of these money metal objects. But when the State establishes a monopoly over money, it has violated the free market's principle of private ownership and exchange.

The free market establishes the quantity of money in circulation, just as it supplies the quantity of consumer goods and capital goods. This raises an important question. Is money a consumer good or a capital good? Or is it neither? I cover this in the Chapter 2: "The Optimum Quantity of Money."

2

THE OPTIMUM QUANTITY OF MONEY

How confident are you that you understand Mises's monetary theory so far? If this were a final exam in a college class on Mises's monetary theory, which answer would you select for the following question: The optimum quantity of money should be determined by . . . "?

A. The national government
B. A national government-licensed central bank
C. A world central bank of central banks
D. The economics department of the University of Chicago
E. The unhampered free market

If you selected E, as Walter Williams says, "Go to the head of the class."

In Chapter 1, we have already explored some implications of Mises's definition of money: *the most marketable commodity*. If money is a commodity, then an analytical question arises: "Is money a consumption good or a production good?" That is, "Is money a form of capital?"

Part I, Chapter 5 of *The Theory of Money and Credit* discusses this issue: "Money as an Economic Good." Mises concluded that money is neither a consumption good nor a capital good. He argued that production and consumption are possible without money (p. 82). Money facilitates both production and consumption, but it is neither a production good nor a consumption good. Money is therefore a *separate analytical category*.

Mises singled out his teacher and co-founder of the Austrian School of economics, Eugen von Böhm-Bawerk, as having erred in designating money as a capital good; he viewed it as social capital (p. 83). Mises disagreed. "It is illegitimate to compare the part played by money in production with that played by ships and railways. Money is obviously not a 'commercial tool' in the same sense as account books, exchange lists, the Stock Exchange, or the credit system" (p. 83).

CHANGES IN THE MONEY SUPPLY

We now come to another crucial aspect of Mises's theory of money. Indeed, it is a uniquely distinguishing feature of his monetary theory, one that is not shared by other modern schools of economic thought. Because money is not capital, he concluded that *an increase of the money supply confers no identifiable social value*. If you fail to understand this point, you will not be able to understand the rest of Mises's theory of money. On this assessment of the value of money, his whole theory of money hinges.

> What prevents us nevertheless from reckoning money among these distribution goods and so among production goods (and incidentally the same objection applies to its inclusion among consumption goods) is the following consideration. The loss of a consumption good or production good results in a loss of human satisfaction; it makes mankind poorer. The gain of such a good results in an improvement of the human economic position; it makes mankind richer. The same cannot be said of the loss or gain of money. Both changes in the available quantity of production goods or consumption

> goods and changes in the available quantity of money involve changes in values; but whereas the changes in the value of the production goods and consumption goods do not mitigate the loss or reduce the gain of satisfaction resulting from the changes in their quantity, the changes in the value of money are accommodated in such a way to the demand for it that, despite increases or decreases in its quantity, the economic position of mankind remains the same. An increase in the quantity of money can no more increase the welfare of the members of a community, than a diminution of it can decrease their welfare. Regarded from this point of view, those goods that are employed as money are indeed what Adam Smith called them—'dead stock, which . . . produces nothing' (p. 85).

Mises went to considerable effort to make his point clear to readers. How much clearer could he have made his position than this? "An increase in the quantity of money can no more increase the welfare of the members of a community, than a diminution of it can decrease their welfare." But he sought to make himself even clearer.

> Production goods derive their value from that of their products. Not so money; for no increase in the welfare of the members of a society can result from the availability of an additional quantity of money. The laws which govern the value of money are different from those which govern the value of production goods and from those which govern the value of consumption goods (p. 86).

This theory regarding the impact that changes in the money supply have on social value is the basis of everything that follows. Mises offered here a unique assessment of the demand for money. He implied here that an individual's demand for production goods or consumption goods, when met by increased production, confers an increase in social value or social welfare.

Both the consumer and the producer are made better off by the exchange. Society is better off because at least two of its members are better off. What Mises inescapably was saying here is this: while an individual wants more money, and a producer of gold can make a profit by selling him more money (gold), *society as a whole is not benefited by this voluntary exchange*. This is why money is a separate analytical category in Mises's economic theory.

Let us take this conclusion even further. If a producer benefits society by increasing the production of a non-monetary good, later finding a buyer, then society is benefitted because there are at least two winners and no losers. (To say this, the economist logically must dismiss as socially irrelevant the negative assessments of envious people who resent anyone else's success.) Therefore, if a producer of gold and a buyer of gold both benefit from an exchange—which they do, or else they would not trade—yet society receives no social benefit, then the analyst has to conclude that some other members of society have been made, or will be made, worse off by the increase in the money supply. This analysis would also apply to decreases in the money supply.

There are two conceptually related issues here: (1) money as a separate analytical category, neither a consumption good nor a production good; (2) changes in the money supply as conveying neither an increase nor decrease in social value.

This leads us to a major question for all economic analysis: "What is social value?"

SUBJECTIVE UTILITY AND SOCIAL VALUE

Mises began his economic analysis with the presupposition that all economic value is subjective. He followed Menger on this point. But if all economic value is subjective, then it cannot be measured by any objective standard. He said this specifically: there is no measure of economic value. This is a major theme in Chapter 2 of *The Theory of Money and Credit*, and it remained a constant throughout his career. (In 1955, Hayek went so far as to write of Mises that "most peculiarities of his views which at first strike many readers as strange and unacceptable are due to the fact that in the consistent development of the subjectivist approach he has for a long time moved ahead of his contemporaries." *The Counter-Revolution of Science*, Part One, note 24.)

If there is no objective measure of an individual's subjective value, then there is no way to make comparisons of subjective utility among individuals. There is no way to add or subtract subjective utility. An individual can *compare* his own subjective utilities on his scale of economic values—first, second, third—but he cannot *measure* them. Even less plausible is any assertion that an outside observer can measure the subjective utilities of others.

The first economist to discuss this in detail was Lionel Robbins, a disciple of Mises's who wrote the Introduction to the 1934 English edition of *Theory of Money and Credit*. In Chapter VI of his book, *An Essay on the Nature and Significance of Economic Science* (1932), Robbins discussed the problem of the epistemological impossibility of making interpersonal comparisons of subjective utilities.

By the time *Human Action* was published, Mises recognized the implications of Robbins's argument for any concept of social value. Mises modified his earlier statement regarding the effects on social value of changes in the supply of money. Once again, he discussed cash-induced changes in the purchasing power of money. He arrived at a different conclusion regarding social value.

> Under these assumptions all that cash-induced changes in purchasing power bring about are shifts in the disposition of wealth among different individuals. Some get richer, others poorer; some are better supplied, others less; what some people gain is paid for by the loss of others. It would, however, be impermissible to interpret this fact by saying that total satisfaction

> remained unchanged or that, while no changes have occurred in total supply, the state of total satisfaction or the sum of happiness has been increased or decreased by changes in the distribution of wealth. It is impossible to discover a standard for comparing the different degrees of satisfaction or happiness attained by various individuals (p. 417).

Nothing can be said of aggregate social value, except this: it cannot be measured. This conclusion is consistent with the assumption of an exclusively subjective theory of economic value. An economist who is consistent in his application of subjective value theory cannot accept even the theoretical possibility of a scientific rationale for making interpersonal comparisons of subjective utility. With respect to aggregate social value—"total satisfaction or total happiness"—the subjectivist can logically say only this: no one on earth can measure it.

NO NEW MONEY IS REQUIRED

On the very next page of *Human Action*, Mises discussed the free market's use of whatever quantity of money is presently in circulation. "As the operation of the market tends to determine the final state of money's purchasing power at the height at which the supply of and the demand for money coincide, there can never be an excess or deficiency of money. Each individual and all individuals together always enjoy fully the advantages which they can derive from indirect exchange and the use of money, no matter whether the total quantity of money is great or small." The conclusion is obvious, and he made it: "The quantity of money available in the whole economy is always sufficient to secure for everybody all that money does and can do" (p. 418).

I emphasize this because there are economic commentators and analysts who claim to represent Mises's position on monetary theory, but who are proponents of the expansion of money by the State or by the fractional reserve banking system. They argue that society can and does benefit from such an expansion of money. Make no mistake about this: *anyone who argues that a change in the money supply conveys either net social benefits or net social costs has repudiated Mises's explicit statement to the contrary in his earlier writings, and has repudiated Mises's denial in his later writings regarding anyone's ability to make such a scientific judgment.* He who defends, in the name of Mises, government or central bank policies that deliberately promote either monetary inflation or monetary deflation has two obligations: (1) to show why his recommended policy is really consistent with Mises's economic theory; (2) to suggest reasons that led Mises to make such a serious mistake about the implications of his own theory.

Mises was in favor of free markets. He did not recommend civil laws against voluntary exchange. Therefore, he did not oppose gold mining. He did not recommend that the State prohibit miners from adding to the quantity of money. But he readily acknowledged that any increase of the money supply from gold mining will inflict losses on some participants in the economy—participants who were not parties in the original transaction of selling new gold into the economy. In this sense, *changes in the money supply cannot be neutral.* There will inevitably be winners and losers.

Mises stressed the following fact in his theory of money: *new money enters an economy at specific points, i.e., through specific voluntary exchanges.* New money does not appear magically in equal percentages in all people's bank accounts or under their mattresses. Money spreads unevenly, and this process has varying effects on individuals, depending on whether they receive early or late access to the new money. This was one of Mises's original contributions to monetary theory, one that is ignored by all other schools of economic analysis.

> An increase in a community's stock of money always means an increase in the amount of money held by a number of economic agents, whether these are the issuers of fiat or credit money or the producers of the substance

> of which commodity money is made. For these persons, the ratio between the demand for money and the stock of it is altered; they have a relative superfluity of money and a relative shortage of other economic goods. The immediate consequence of both circumstances is that the marginal utility to them of the monetary unit diminishes. This necessarily influences their behavior in the market. They are in a stronger position as buyers. They will now express in the market their demand for the objects they desire more intensively than before; they are able to offer more money for the commodities that they wish to acquire. It will be the obvious result of this that the prices of the goods concerned will rise, and that the objective exchange value of money will fall in comparison.
>
> But this rise of prices will by no means be restricted to the market for those goods that are desired by those who originally have the new money at their disposal. In addition, those who have brought these goods to market will have their incomes and their proportionate stocks of money increased and, in their turn, will be in a position to demand more intensively the goods they want, so that these goods will also rise in price. Thus the increase of prices continues, having a diminishing effect, until all commodities, some to a greater and some to a lesser extent, are reached by it.
>
> The increase in the quantity of money does not mean an increase of income for all individuals. On the contrary, those sections of the community that are the last to be reached by the additional quantity of money have their incomes reduced, as a consequence of the decrease in the value of money called forth by the increase in its quantity; this will be referred to later (*TM&C*, p. 139).

This analysis of the *uneven spread of new money* applies to gold as well as to central bank money. It therefore applies to a legally unrestricted free market.

Let us, for instance, suppose that a new gold mine is opened in an isolated state. The supplementary quantity of gold that streams from it into commerce goes at first to the owners of the mine and then by turns to those who have dealings with them. If we schematically divide the whole community into four groups, the mine owners, the producers of luxury goods, the remaining producers, and the agriculturalists, the first two groups will be able to enjoy the benefits resulting from the reduction in the value of money the former of them to a greater extent than the latter. But even as soon as we reach the third group, the situation is altered. The profit obtained by this group as a result of the increased demands of the first two will already be offset to some extent by the rise in the prices of luxury goods which will have experienced the full effect of the depreciation by the time it begins to affect other goods. Finally for the fourth group, the whole process will result in nothing but loss. The farmers will have to pay dearer for all industrial products before they are compensated by the increased prices of agricultural products. It is true that when at last the prices of agricultural products do rise, the period of economic hardship for the farmers is over; but it will no longer be possible for them to secure profits that will compensate them for the losses they have suffered. That is to say, they will not be able to use their increased receipts to purchase commodities at prices corresponding to the old level of the value of money; for the increase of prices will already have gone through the whole community. Thus the losses suffered by the farmers at the time when they still sold their products at the old low prices but had to pay for the products of others at the new and higher prices remain uncompensated. It is these losses of the groups that are the last to be reached by the variation in the value of money which ultimately constitute the source of the profits made by the mine owners and the groups most closely connected with them (pp. 208–9).

The later recipients of the new gold that has entered the economy face higher prices than would otherwise have prevailed, had the new gold not been mined and spent into circulation by mine owners. These late recipients were not parties to the early transactions, beginning with the mine owners, who sold the gold either for gold coins or money-certificates, and who then spent it. Nevertheless, these late recipients suffer losses.

Mises said specifically that the sources of the economic profits of the gold mine owner are the economic losses sustained by the late recipients of the new gold. "It is these losses of the groups that are the last to be reached by the variation in the value of money which ultimately constitute the source of the profits made by the mine owners and the groups most closely connected with them." This indicates a fundamental aspect of Mises's monetary theory that is rarely mentioned: *the expansion or contraction of money is a zero-sum game*. Mises did not use this terminology, but he used the zero-sum concept. Because the free market always maximizes the utility of the existing money supply, changes in the money supply inescapably have the characteristic features of a zero-sum game. Some individuals are made better off by an increase in the money supply; others are made worse off. The existing money is an example of a "fixed pie of social value." Adding to the money supply does not add to its value.

Economists argue that in a conventional economic exchange, both parties win. One person does not benefit at the expense of another unless there has been fraud. The "pie of social value" has grown because there are two winners. The conceptual problem begins with a fixed social pie.

Mises argued that the losses of the late-coming losers are the source of income for the early arrival winners. This inescapably identifies the monetary system as a zero-sum game. In *Human Action*, he included a section denying what he calls the Montaigne dogma: "*the gain of one man is the damage of another; no man profits but at the loss of other*" (p. 660). He then added: "Now the Montaigne dogma is true with regard to the effects of cash-induced changes in the purchasing power of money on deferred payments." He was being disingenuous here, which is not characteristic of his argumentation generally. The three words, "on deferred payments," appear to restrict the applicability of the Montaigne dogma in monetary affairs. Yet his entire theory of money rests on this dogma's complete applicability in the matter of increases and decreases in the money supply. The economic benefits obtained by the early users of new money, even gold, are made at the expense of those who gain access to it after it has altered the array of prices. (Although he never described the reverse scenario, deflation, he would have said that losses suffered by losers of credit-money that has disappeared through default must be the source of the economic gains for holders of coins or currency or credit money that did not perish in the deflation, who soon will face lower money prices because of the contraction of the money supply.)

Again, here is his theory, briefly stated. Money is neither a production good nor a consumption good. Thus, increases or decreases in the supply of money cannot scientifically be said to create or destroy wealth in general. These changes distribute wealth.

This raises a major epistemological issue. If the economist cannot logically say anything about net social utility, because he cannot scientifically make interpersonal comparisons of subjective utilities, then he cannot identify a zero-sum game. Scientifically speaking, given the individualistic epistemology of subjective economic value theory, no one can say whether a game's redistribution of wealth among its participants has increased or decreased or failed to change net social value. Perhaps the loser really does not mind, and the winner is ecstatic, or vice versa. If we are strict subjectivists, we must refrain from using the idea of a zero-sum game. It is not that Montaigne was wrong about capitalism. It is that his dogma cannot apply to any exchange. We cannot legitimately make interpersonal comparisons of subjective utilities if we hold to an exclusively subjectivist value theory.

A subjective value theory economist can, however, legitimately deny another subjective value theory economist's assertion that a transaction is or is not part of a zero-sum game. He can also legitimately deny that someone who suggests a policy of either inflation or deflation has scientific grounds for justifying his recommendation in terms of any alleged benefits to society. In short, the power of exclusively subjective value theory is very great in undermining all policy recommendations that are based exclusively on subjective value theory. But, like an acid that eats everything, including every known container, it is a risky argument to invoke.

GOLD STANDARD VS. STATE-ISSUED MONEY

Mises's commitment to economic freedom led him to the conclusion that the State should not prohibit gold mining and silver mining, for these are voluntary activities. But he did argue for market-created monetary standards that are based on money metals. Why? Because the cost of mining is high, which will always limit the expansion of money. In the Preface to the 1934 English edition of *Theory of Money and Credit*, he wrote:

> Under the gold standard, the determination of the value of money is dependent upon the profitability of gold production. To some, this may appear a disadvantage; and it is certain that it introduces an incalculable factor into economic activity. Nevertheless, it does not lay the prices of commodities open to violent and sudden changes from the monetary side. The biggest variations in the value of money that we have experienced during the last century have originated not in the circumstances of gold production, but in the policies of governments and banks-of-issue. Dependence of the value of money on the production of gold does at least mean its independence of the politics of the hour.

> The dissociation of the currencies from a definitive and unchangeable gold parity has made the value of money a plaything of politics (pp. 17–18).

It is obvious what Mises regarded as the supreme benefit of a gold standard: *a metallic money standard hampers the State.* In his chapter on "Monetary Policy," he wrote:

> The significance of adherence to a metallic-money system lies in the freedom of the value of money from state influence that such a system guarantees. Beyond doubt, considerable disadvantages are involved in the fact that not only fluctuations in the ratio of the supply of money and the demand for it, but also fluctuations in the conditions of production of the metal and variations in the industrial demand for it, exert an influence on the determination of the value of money. It is true that these effects, in the case of gold (and even in the case of silver), are not immoderately great, and these are the only two monetary metals that need be considered in modern times. But even if the effects were greater, such a money would still deserve preference over one subject to state intervention, since the latter sort of money would be subject to still greater fluctuations (p. 238).

He said it over and over: metallic money is superior to money issued by the State. Its value will fluctuate less than State-issued money, but it will fluctuate. A monetary system that cannot provide stable prices is the price which men must pay for economic liberty, namely, freedom from the control of money by the State. With the State in control of money, society gets more fluctuations in value and less freedom.

Mises recognized the costs associated with gold mining. He discussed this in Part III, Chapter III, "Fiduciary Media and the Demand for Money." He said that capital and labor must be applied to mining. This reduces productivity in other areas of the economy. Also, precious metals that are used for money cannot be used to satisfy industrial or ornamental demand for these metals, further reducing welfare. He even said that, apart from successful voluntary ways to reduce demand for metallic money, "the welfare of the community would have been reduced" by the costs of mining (p. 299). Even the great Mises sometimes could not retain his commitment to subjective value theory, with its concomitant denial of community welfare.

Mises favored credit clearing-house systems (p. 297). They lower the demand for money, i.e., reduce the downward competitive pressure on money-denominated prices. A clearing house produces "the reciprocal cancellation of claims to money" (p. 283). For a fee, a bank clearing house offsets daily liabilities and assets that are created as a result of commerce. Business A owes business B ten ounces of gold. Business B owes business C ten ounces of gold. Business C owes business A ten ounces of gold. So, at the end of the day, the accounts are cleared, and no gold changes ownership if the three firms belong to the same clearing house. There can also be clearing houses for clearing houses. This arrangement is voluntary and not dependent on the expansion of money, either metallic or fiduciary. It therefore saves on capital and labor that would otherwise have been devoted to mining for the purpose of digging up money metals.

Why did Mises defend a money system based on money metals? First, because such a system reduces fluctuations in the value of money. Second, in order to get the State out of the money business. The State makes things worse.

The State's policy-makers are unable to foresee the results of their interventions in the money supply. They are blind. The free market is preferable to the State in the establishing of the optimum supply of money.

> The results of our investigation into the development and significance of monetary policy should not surprise us. That the state, after having for a period used the power which it nowadays has of influencing to some

> extent the determination of the objective exchange value of money in order to affect the distribution of income, should have to abandon its further exercise, will not appear strange to those who have a proper appreciation of the economic function of the state in that social order which rests upon private property in the means of production. The state does not govern the market; in the market in which products are exchanged it may quite possibly be a powerful party, but nevertheless it is only one party of many, nothing more than that. All its attempts to transform the exchange ratios between economic goods that are determined in the market can only be undertaken with the instruments of the market. It can never foresee exactly what the result of any particular intervention will be. It cannot bring about a desired result in the degree that it wishes, because the means that the influencing of demand and supply place at its disposal only affect the pricing process through the medium of the subjective valuations of individuals; but no judgment as to the intensity of the resulting transformation of these valuations can be made except when the intervention is a small one, limited to one or a few groups of commodities of lesser importance, and even in such a case only approximately. All monetary policies encounter the difficulty that the effects of any measures taken in order to influence the fluctuations of the objective exchange value of money can neither be foreseen in advance, nor their nature and magnitude be determined even after they have already occurred (pp. 238–39).

First, Mises was convinced that the free market always maximizes the use of the existing money supply. No additional money is needed, even though each participant would like more money for himself. Second, he was convinced that mining costs establish limits to the expansion of money. This is an advantage, for all monetary inflation has unforeseeable effects on the distribution of wealth: winners and losers. If mine owners make a profit by producing metals, some of which will be used for money, then others in the economy suffer losses as a result of this increase in the money supply. A metallic money standard minimizes these losses. Conclusion: a metallic money standard is therefore preferable to any State-run system in which the State has the power to increase or decrease the money supply or set exchange rates for money. As he wrote in a chapter of his 1951 appendix, "The Principle of Sound Money,"

> The excellence of the gold standard is to be seen in the fact that it renders the determination of the monetary unit's purchasing power independent of the policies of governments and political parties. Furthermore, it prevents rulers from eluding the financial and budgetary prerogatives of the representative assemblies. Parliamentary control of finances works only if the government is not in a position to provide for unauthorized expenditures by increasing the circulating amount of fiat money. Viewed in this light, the gold standard appears as an indispensable implement of the body of constitutional guarantees that make the system of representative government function (p. 416).

Mises recognized the implications of a State-induced redistribution of wealth. The following comment came in his discussion of State-issued money. In *Human Action*, he wrote:

> If the government-made cash-induced changes in the purchasing power of money resulted only in shifts of wealth from some people to other people, it would not be permissible to condemn them from the point of view of catallactics' [economic theory's] scientific neutrality. It is obviously fraudulent to justify them under the pretext of the commonweal or public welfare. But one could still consider them as political measures suitable to promote the interests of some groups of people at the expense of others without further detriment (p. 428).

Mises always defended his economic analysis as value-free. Here, he acknowledged that monetary inflation by the State does redistribute wealth. It would be fraudulent, he said, for politicians to justify the issue of additional fiat money on the basis of the supposed increases in the public welfare. Why fraudulent? Because, for Mises (and for any fully consistent subjective value theorist), *there is no such thing as measurable public welfare*. It is impossible to add up benefits and losses in estimating total welfare because there is no objective measure of subjective utility. So, any State policy that rests on a claim of an increase in the public welfare is scientifically bogus and therefore fraudulent.

This is a radical epistemological position to defend. It means at least two things: (1) a subjective economist cannot scientifically recommend any policy on the basis of increased aggregate social welfare; (2) any appeal to a supposed increase in aggregate public welfare must rest on some version of a theory of objective economic value.

Mises nevertheless concluded, "But one could still consider them [cash-induced redistributions of wealth] as political measures suitable to promote the interests of some groups of people at the expense of others without further detriment." Here is a major point of contention between Rothbard and Mises. Rothbard regarded the State as morally evil because its effects always redistribute wealth by coercion. He had a moral objection to the State that Mises never voiced. Therefore, his objection to the State's fiat currency had a moral element. But he would have agreed with Mises on this point: it is fraudulent for politicians to justify an expansion of State-issued money on the basis of any supposed increase of public welfare.

MISES VS. GOVERNMENT MONETARY POLICY

Mises believed in free market-generated money. He believed that the civil government should not have any monetary policy, other than an absolutely fixed money supply. A civil government that is powerful enough to have a flexible, "scientific" monetary policy is too powerful, in Mises's opinion. As he wrote in his 1951 appendix essay, "The Return to Sound Money,"

> The first step must be a radical and unconditional abandonment of any further inflation. The total amount of dollar bills, whatever their name or legal characteristic may be, must not be increased by further issuance. No bank must be permitted to expand the total amount of its deposits subject to check or the balance of such deposits of any individual customer, be he a private citizen or the U.S. Treasury, otherwise than by receiving cash deposits in legal-tender banknotes from the public or by receiving a check payable by another domestic bank subject to the same limitations. This means a rigid 100 percent reserve for all future deposits; i.e., all deposits not already in existence on the first day of the reform (p. 448).

In *Human Action*, Mises said that the government's task is to enforce contracts. Among these contracts are contracts for redeeming money-certificates for money metals on demand. He defined a money-certificate as a receipt for a money metal that has 100 percent of the promised metal in reserve. He said that banks should not be favored by the government. They should not be allowed the right to break contracts, which is what a refusal to redeem money-certificates on demand is. "What is needed to prevent any further credit expansion is to place the banking business under the general rules of commercial and civil laws compelling every individual to fulfill all obligations in full compliance with the terms of the contract" (p. 440).

A traditional gold standard is where the government issues pieces of paper that promise to the bearer full redemption in gold coins. Mises did not defend the traditional gold standard. His theory of money and credit denies the legitimacy of such a gold standard. Mises did not believe that civil governments should be in any way involved in the creation of money or the destruction of money. He defended free banking because he did not trust the government with sufficient authority to enforce 100 percent reserve banking.

He believed that a non-governmental national gold standard is no different in principle or operation from the international gold standard. There was no one-world government that enforced the international gold standard when he wrote *Human Action* or in the nineteenth century, when it was a major factor in world trade. In fact, the attempt by modern governments to regulate in any way an international gold standard is always a political ruse to undermine its anti-inflationary bias. "The international gold standard works without any action on the part of governments. It is effective real cooperation of all members of the world-embracing market community. . . . What governments call international monetary cooperation is concerted action for the sake of credit expansion" (p. 473). Conclusion: *there is no need for a national government to enforce a national gold standard*.

Economic logic does not end or begin at a political border. There are no economic laws linking individuals within borders that do not also apply to individuals across borders. To argue that there are different economic laws for different groups is utterly spurious. Mises called this dualism *polylogism*. He devoted an entire section of *Human Action* to its refutation (Chapter 3). (I believe that the only term that was more contemptible than "polylogist" in Mises's vocabulary was "empiricist." But I could be wrong. Maybe "polylogist" was at the top.)

To argue that Mises recommended any monetary policy for governments is to argue that he simultaneously believed that (1) the international gold standard needs no joint government intervention; (2) nevertheless, for some unstated reason, domestic governments must develop and enforce specific monetary policies relating to gold, banks, and the issue of government claims to money. But Mises did not hold such a polylogist position. Mises left no wiggle room on this point: "Now, the gold standard is not a game, but a social institution. Its working does not depend on the preparedness of any people to observe arbitrary rules. It is controlled by the operation of inexorable economic law" (p. 459).

I remind you once again of the representative "conservative" policy recommendation that I mentioned in Chapter 1.

> There is nothing more important that the government can provide individual producers than a reliable standard of value, a unit of account that retains its constancy as a measuring device.

This idea is a conservative's well-intentioned but totally anti-Misesian version of a comment by John Maynard Keynes, in his book, *Essays in Persuasion* (1931):

> The Individualistic Capitalism of today, precisely because it entrusts saving to the individual investor and production to the individual employer, presumes a stable measuring-rod of value, and cannot be efficient—perhaps cannot survive—without one.
>
> For these grave causes we must free ourselves from the deep distrust which exists against allowing the regulation of the standard of value to be the subject of *deliberate decision*. We can no longer afford to leave it in the category which the distinguishing characteristics are possessed in different degrees by the weather, the birth-rate, and the Constitution,—matters which are settled by natural causes, or are the resultant of the separate action of many individuals acting independently, or required a Revolution to change them.

Mises recommended no "scientific" government monetary policy whatsoever. He recommended private ownership, the State's enforcement of all contracts, and legal sanctions against private violence. As he wrote in his 1927 book, *Liberalismus*, "This is the function that the liberal doctrine assigns to the state: the protection of property, liberty, and peace" (*Liberalism in the Classical Tradition* [1985], p. 37). Providing money of stable purchasing power was not on the list. He took this extremely limited set of government policies and applied them to all of economics, including monetary theory.

CONCLUSION

Money is neither a production good nor a consumption good. Therefore, an increase or decrease of the money supply cannot be said to add to the social value of the economy. There is no way to measure social value.

Mises said that profits from mining are paid for by those participants in the economy who gain access to the newly mined money metal late in the process of exchange, after prices have risen. Those who gain early access are the beneficiaries.

He defended the metallic money standard because it reduces fluctuations in the value of money compared to State-issued money. The costs of mining are greater than the cost of printing money. This reduces the increase of money. For this reason, a precious metal-based monetary system is an advantage over a State-issued currency. He recommended private ownership and the State's enforcement of contracts. He did not offer any recommended monetary policy for the State, other than a freeze on its existing money supply.

Then what of the goal of stable prices? What of the goal of a truly neutral money, in which changes in the money supply hurt no one? These are the subjects of Chapter 3.

3
TWO MYTHS: NEUTRAL MONEY AND STABLE PRICES

There are two myths in the monetary field, according to Mises: the myth of neutral money and the myth of the stable price level. His monetary theory avoided both of them.

NEUTRAL MONEY

In the chapter on "Indirect Exchange"—money—in *Human Action*, Mises begins Section 2, "Observations on Some Widespread Errors," with this observation: "There is first of all the spurious idea of the supposed neutrality of money" (p. 395). The price effects of new money spread unevenly when it enters an economy. I have already discussed this unique aspect of Mises's theory of money in Chapter 2. Neutral money is money that is generated by a monetary system in which there are no involuntary wealth-redistribution effects inflicted on third parties when there are changes in the supply of money.

Mises was an advocate of market-generated money, both in theory and in practice: my point in Chapter 1. He did not believe that any government agency or committee could design and operate a monetary system that would avoid the problems associated with wealth redistribution from those who gain access to new money late in the process to those who gained access early. He believed that the unhampered free market minimizes these effects by imposing high costs on mining, thereby reducing the flow of new money into the economy. A metallic money system, he believed, would reduce fluctuations in the value of money. This would also make accurate predictions less costly regarding the price of goods in relation to money. He wrote in *Human Action*:

> As money can never be neutral and stable in purchasing power, a government's plans concerning the determination of the quantity of money can never be impartial and fair to all members of society. Whatever a government does in the pursuit of aims to influence the height of purchasing power depends necessarily on the rulers' personal value judgments. It always furthers the interests of some groups of people at the expense of other groups. It never serves what is called the commonweal or the public welfare. In the field of monetary policies, there is no such thing as a scientific ought.
>
> The choice of the good to be employed as a medium of exchange and as money is never indifferent. It determines the course of the cash-induced changes in purchasing power. The question is only who should make the choice: the people buying and selling on the market, or the government? It was the market which in a selective process, going on for ages, finally assigned to the precious metals gold and silver the character of money (p. 419).

There are two objections to a government-operated money system. First, governments choose monetary policies in terms of the personal value judgments of the responsible decision-makers. Second, these decision-makers cannot accurately foresee the long-term effects of their monetary policies. Mises wrote in *The Theory of Money and Credit*:

> The State does not govern the market; in the market in which products are exchanged it may quite possibly

> be a powerful party, but nevertheless it is only one party of many, nothing more than that. All its attempts to transform the exchange ratios between economic goods that are determined in the market can only be undertaken with the instruments of the market. It can never foresee exactly what the result of any particular intervention will be. It cannot bring about a desired result in the degree that it wishes, because the means that the influencing of demand and supply place at its disposal only affect the pricing process through the medium of the subjective valuations of individuals; but no judgment as to the intensity of the resulting transformation of these valuations can be made except when the intervention is a small one, limited to one or a few groups of commodities of lesser importance, and even in such a case only approximately. All monetary policies encounter the difficulty that the effects of any measures taken in order to influence the fluctuations of the objective exchange value of money can neither be foreseen in advance, nor their nature and magnitude be determined even after they have already occurred (pp. 238–39).

Mises believed that an unhampered free market is likely to produce a slowly rising money supply and slowly falling prices. These effects seem to be antitheses of each other. Was he predicting inflationary recession? Deflationary prosperity? What?

DEFINING INFLATION AND DEFLATION

The latest and by far the simplest statement by Mises regarding his definition of inflation was made at a seminar sponsored by the University of Chicago Law School in 1951. "Inflation, as the term was always used everywhere and especially in this country, means increasing the quantity of money and bank notes in circulation and the quantity of bank deposits subject to check." (*Economic Freedom and Intervention: An Anthology of Articles and Essays by Ludwig von Mises*, 1990, p. 99.) He went on: "But people today use the term 'inflation' to refer to the phenomenon that is an inevitable consequence of inflation, that is the tendency of all prices and wage rates to rise." This was very close to his definition in *Human Action*: "What many people today call inflation or deflation is no longer the great increase or decrease in the supply of money, but its inexorable consequences, the general tendency toward a rise or a fall in commodity prices and wage rates" (p. 420).

In *Theory of Money and Credit*, he went out of his way to avoid defining inflation and deflation. "Observant readers may perhaps be struck by the fact that in this book no precise definition as given of the terms Inflation and Deflation (or Restriction or Contraction); that they are in fact hardly employed at all, and then only in places where nothing in particular depends upon their precision" (p. 239). Thus, anyone who relies on his earlier definitions of these terms necessarily involves himself in imprecision—a deliberate imprecision that Mises self-consciously adopted in that book. Here is his imprecise definition, which raised the theoretically peripheral issue of a goods-induced price competition:

> In theoretical investigation there is only one meaning that can rationally be attached to the expression inflation: an increase in the quantity of money (in the broader sense of the term, so as to include fiduciary media as well), that is not offset by a corresponding increase in the need for money (again in the broader sense of the term), so that a fall in the objective exchange value of money must occur. Again, deflation (or restriction, or contraction) signifies a diminution of the quantity of money (in the broader sense) which is not offset by a corresponding diminution of the demand for money (in the broader sense), so that an increase in the objective exchange value of money must occur. If we so define these concepts, it follows that either inflation or deflation is constantly going on, for a situation in which the objective exchange value of money did not alter could hardly ever exist for very long.

> The theoretical value of our definition is not in the least reduced by the fact that we are not able to measure the fluctuations in the objective exchange value of money, or even by the fact that we are not able to discern them at all except when they are large (p. 240).

The problem with this definition is that it ignores the heart of his theory of the uneven spread of new money, namely, that any increase or decrease in the money supply must produce uneven price effects through time. When there is an increase in the money supply, new money appears at specific points in the economy. Early users of the new money spend it before their competitors are aware of the new conditions of supply and demand. They buy at yesterday's prices, which generally prevail today. Rival consumers are unaware of the increase in the supply of money. But, as the information regarding the new conditions of money supply—higher bids in terms of money—spreads to more market participants, they lower the marginal value of money in their personal value scales, and they raise the marginal value of non-monetary goods and services. They bid additional money, so prices rise. Those participants who gain access later suffer a loss of purchasing power, whether or not market prices have risen. These prices would otherwise have fallen. There is no way that an increase of supply of money will not have price effects. Mises's later definition of inflation is consistent with his theory of changes in the money supply in the economy. His definition in 1912 (1924) was not clearly consistent with his theory. Fortunately, he warned readers of its imprecision. Those who regard themselves as Misesians should honor this warning. They should adopt his later definition.

SLOWLY FALLING PRICES

The second myth that Mises exposed is the myth of stable prices. Mises's case for free market money is the case for relatively slow and predictable increases in the money supply. There are two main sources of these increases in a free market economy: the output of mines and the expansion of credit fiduciary money in a free banking system.

Mises did not call for the legislative prohibition of all gold and silver mining, nor did he call for 100 percent reserve banking as a legislative requirement, as I explain in Chapter 4. He did not trust the civil government enough to empower it to this degree. "The concept of money as a creature of Law and the State is clearly untenable. It is not justified by a single phenomenon of the market. To ascribe to the State the power of dictating the laws of exchange, is to ignore the fundamental principles of money-using society" (*TM&C*, p. 69).

In a growing economy, Mises argued, the division of labor is increasing. The market's specialization of production is therefore also increasing. Population also may be growing. Under such conditions, "there prevails a tendency toward an increase in the demand for money. Additional people appear on the scene and want to establish cash holdings" (*Human Action*, p. 411). Economic self-sufficiency is replaced by dependence on the market, which is a market identified by the use of money. "Thus the price-raising tendency emanating from what is called the 'normal' gold production encounters a price-cutting tendency emanating from the increased demand for cash holding" (p. 411). These two tendencies do not neutralize each other. They are separate phenomena. "Both processes take their own course . . ." (pp. 411–12). The gold from the mines moves into the economy, one transaction at a time.

When we say that there is an increase in the demand for cash balances, this is another way of saying an increase in bids for money. Those people with goods or services to exchange enter the market and offer them for sale. If the money supply is relatively stable, those with items for sale must offer more for the money they want to obtain. In the auction for money, higher bids appear. "Higher bids *for* money" is another way of saying "lower bids *in* money." Sellers of goods (buyers of money) offer more goods at yesterday's prices. Prices denominated in money go down = prices denominated in goods go up.

More goods and services are available for purchase. This means that there has been an increase of choices available to people per unit of currency at the newer, lower prices. Probably the best definition of "increase in wealth" is "increase of choices." As Mises said, "such a fall in money prices does not in the least impair the benefits derived from the additional wealth produced" (p. 428). This is not deflation, as he defined it later in his career. This is price competition.

Had he been aware of the historical statistics, Mises no doubt would have made good use of the example of the falling price of computing power since 1965. It is not likely that any economist would want to present a theoretical case for a theory that the world has been made poorer by the fall in the prices of computers. What engineer would turn in his multifunction, solar-powered, scientific $20 calculator in order to go back to a slide rule? ("Where was that decimal point supposed to go?") This steady drop in the price of computing power has been going on since at least 1910. Computing speed per dollar doubled every three years (1910–1950), then every two years (1950–1965), and then every year (1966–2000). Nothing in human history has matched this reduction in price (increase in output) at such a rate for so long a period. But the fact that such a steady increase in consumer value is both possible and economically profitable to producers indicates that there is no need for an increase in the money supply to facilitate exchanges. This price-cutting process is not a defect of the free market economy; it is a benefit. Mises said, that "one must not say that a fall in prices caused by an increase in the production of the goods concerned is proof of some disequilibrium which cannot be eliminated otherwise than by increasing the quantity of money" (p. 428).

Economists define scarcity as "an excess of demand over supply at zero price." The goal of production, economists assure us, is to increase consumption. Put differently, the goal is to reduce scarcity. Put differently again, the goal is to approach the price of zero as a limit for all scarce economic resources. The goal of production, in short, is to achieve constantly falling prices. Yet only Mises and his disciples defend this outcome of a free market monetary order coupled with capitalism's productivity: falling prices.

In this sense, the Misesians are the true macro-economists. Their theory of the autonomous ("endogenous") entrepreneurial market process is consistent with their theory of an integrated, coherent outcome. The market does not require intervention by the State's economic planners or by its licensed monopolistic agency, the central bank. All other schools of economic opinion recommend monetary inflation as the only way to overcome increased productivity's outcome in the macro economy—falling prices—which they proclaim as the goal of production at the micro level: falling prices. They do not believe that the free market endogenously supplies the correct quantity of money to facilitate voluntary exchange. They see macroeconomics as fundamentally inconsistent with microeconomics. They want Big Brother and the holding company (the central bank) to supply new money scientifically, so that the market pricing process can function properly. This is true of the Keynesians, the monetarists, and the supply-siders. None of them trusts the free market in the area of monetary policy.

If output is rising in a free market, and the money supply is fairly constant, then prices will fall. The market's clearing price is that price which allows a sale in which there are no further buyers or sellers at the sale price. The high bid wins. When output is rising, buyers of money (sellers of goods) increase their bids by offering more goods for sale at the old price. This is another way of saying that prices denominated in money fall, or at least do not rise as high as they would otherwise have risen, had there been no increase in the quantity of goods and services offered for sale. Mises described this process in his

1951 addition to *Theory of Money and Credit*, in the essay titled, "The Principle of Sound Money." He spoke of "a general tendency of money prices and money wages to drop" (p. 417). This is not deflation, which Mises defined as a decrease in the quantity of money and bank notes in circulation and the quantity of bank deposits subject to check. Price competition is not deflation.

In a free market, there cannot be either stable prices or stable money. Conditions of supply and demand keep changing, including people's tastes and their subjective valuations. There can be a moderately stable supply of free market money. Whether prices in general rise or fall, or which prices rise or fall, is determined by the productivity of the participants in the economy in relation to their demand for cash balances.

If prices fall in a productive economy with free-market money, then the goal of stable prices can be achieved in one of two ways: (1) reduce production; (2) inflate the money supply. Only the advocates of zero economic growth are willing to affirm the first option. The entire economic profession, except for the Misesians, affirms the second. I would go so far as to say that *there is no better litmus test of orthodox Misesianism than a denial of any monetary policy that has stable prices as its goal.* Mises made this clear.

> The ideal of a money with an exchange value that is not subject to variations due to changes in the ratio between the supply of money and the need for it that is, a money with an invariable *innere objektive Tauschwert* [objective exchange-value] demands the intervention of a regulating authority in the determination of the value of money; and its continued intervention. But here immediately most serious doubts arise from the circumstance, already referred to, that we have no useful knowledge of the quantitative significance of given measures intended to influence the value of money. More serious still is the circumstance that we are by no

> means in a position to determine with precision whether variations have occurred in the exchange value of money from any cause whatever, and if so to what extent, quite apart from the question of whether such changes have been effected by influences working from the monetary side. Attempts to stabilize the exchange value of money in this sense must therefore be frustrated at the outset by the fact that both their goal and the road to it are obscured by a darkness that human knowledge will never be able to penetrate. But the uncertainty that would exist as to whether there was any need for intervention to maintain the stability of the exchange value of money, and as to the necessary extent of such intervention, would inevitably give full license again to the conflicting interests of the inflationists and restrictionists. Once the principle is so much as admitted that the state may and should influence the value of money, even if it were only to guarantee the stability of its value, the danger of mistakes and excesses immediately arises again (p. 237).

One more time: "Once the principle is so much as admitted that the state may and should influence the value of money, even if it were only to guarantee the stability of its value, the danger of mistakes and excesses immediately arises again."

MISES VS. INDEX NUMBERS

The idea of a stable price level necessarily involves both the theoretical possibility and the technical requirement of index numbers. To speak of "stable prices" is necessarily to speak of a *representative statistical index* of all prices. Some prices rise. Other prices fall. Others stay the same. The economist who says that the State must supply additional money in order to keep free market prices stable is either calling for a world without change—the denial of history—or else he has in mind a statistical index of prices.

All index numbers lack what true measures require: objectivity and permanence. Mises included a critique of index numbers in *Human Action*. It appears in Chapter 12, "The Sphere of Economic Calculation," Section 4, "Stabilization." He specifically targeted Irving Fisher, the famous Yale University economist who had long promoted government monetary policies to provide stable purchasing power. Fisher became famous after his prediction in September, 1929, that the American stock market was at a permanently high plateau. He lost his personal fortune in the four years that followed. He was the inventer of the Rolodex, a far more useful tool than the index number, which he also invented.

Mises had four criticisms of index numbers. First, they do not measure product quality changes. Second, they do not measure changes in people's valuations, which cause changes in demand and production. Third, they require their creators to assign importance to the various categories of goods and services. This procedure is arbitrary. Fourth, they require the use of averages for the data. There are different methods of doing this. "Each of them leads to different results" (p. 223). "The pretentious solemnity which statisticians and statistical bureaus display in computing indexes of purchasing power and cost of living is out of place. These index numbers are at best rather crude and inaccurate illustrations of changes which have occurred" (p. 223). In the preface to the English edition of *Theory of Money and Credit*, he wrote:

> If it should be thought that index numbers offer us an instrument for providing currency policy with a solid foundation and making it independent of the changing economic programs of governments and political parties, perhaps I may be permitted to refer to what I have said in the present work on the impossibility of singling out any particular method of calculating index numbers as the sole scientifically correct one and calling all the others scientifically wrong. There are many ways

of calculating purchasing power by means of index numbers, and every single one of them is right, from certain tenable points of view; but every single one of them is also wrong, from just as many equally tenable points of view. Since each method of calculation will yield results that are different from those of every other method, and since each result, if it is made the basis of practical measures, will further certain interests and injure others, it is obvious that each group of persons will declare for those methods that will best serve its own interests. At the very moment when the manipulation of purchasing power is declared to be a legitimate concern of currency policy, the question of the level at which this purchasing power is to be fixed will attain the highest political significance. Under the gold standard, the determination of the value of money is dependent upon the profitability of gold production. To some, this may appear a disadvantage; and it is certain that it introduces an incalculable factor into economic activity. Nevertheless, it does not lay the prices of commodities open to violent and sudden changes from the monetary side. The biggest variations in the value of money that we have experienced during the last century have originated not in the circumstances of gold production, but in the policies of governments and banks-of-issue. Dependence of the value of money on the production of gold does at least mean its independence of the politics of the hour. The dissociation of the currencies from a definitive and unchangeable gold parity has made the value of money a plaything of politics. To-day we see considerations of the value of money driving all other considerations into the background in both domestic and international economic policy. We are not very far now from a state of affairs in which 'economic policy' is primarily understood to mean the question of influencing the purchasing power of money (pp. 17–18).

It is not possible to achieve a stable price level in a neutral manner. New money must be spent into circulation at specific points in the economy. The uneven spread of this new money is inescapable. The wealth effects are not equal to all participants in the economy. Mises was adamant: "The notion of neutral money is no less contradictory than that of a stable price level" (*Human Action*, p. 415). "With the real universe of action and unceasing change, with the economic system which cannot be rigid, neither neutrality of money nor stability of its purchasing power are compatible. . . . All plans to render money neutral and stable are contradictory. Money is an element of action and consequently of change" (p. 416).

In his concluding remarks to his book, *Monetary Stabilization and Cyclical Policy* (1928), Mises wrote: "Abandoning the pursuit of the chimera of a money of unchanging purchasing power calls for neither resignation nor disregard of the social consequences of changes in monetary value. The necessary conclusion from this discussion is that the stability of the purchasing power of the monetary unit presumes stability of all exchange relationships and, therefore, the absolute abandonment of the market economy" (Mises, *On the Manipulation of Money and Credit* [1978], p. 107).

The period from 1815 to 1914 was the era of the international gold standard. It was not a pure gold coin standard. Fractional reserve banking did operate. There were booms and busts, which, he taught, were caused by the practices of fractional reserve banks. (See Chapter 5.) But it was a long period of generally stable prices, at least according to some economic historians' index numbers. Prices in 1914 at the outbreak of World War I were about what they were in 1815, at the end of the Napoleonic Wars. Mises explained this price stability in terms of an increase in the money supply. The price-competition associated with an increase in the division of labor was offset in the index by the increase of bank-credit money.

> Economic history shows us a continual increase in the demand for money. The characteristic feature of the development of the demand for money is its intensification; the growth of division of labor and consequently of exchange transactions, which have constantly become more and more indirect and dependent on the use of money, have helped to bring this about, as well as the increase of population and prosperity. The tendencies which result in an increase in the demand for money became so strong in the years preceding the war that even if the increase in the stock of money had been very much greater than it actually was, the objective exchange value of money would have been sure to increase. Only the circumstance that this increase in the demand for money was accompanied by an extraordinarily large expansion of credit, which certainly exceeded the increase in the demand for money in the broader sense, can serve to explain the fact that the objective exchange value of money during this period not only failed to increase, but actually decreased (*TM&C*, p. 151).

CONCLUSION

Mises argued that the unregulated free market makes full use of the existing money supply. Any additional money cannot be said to add social value. Mining adds money, but this cannot be stopped in a free market society. The increase of the money supply through mining is slow and relatively predictable. Unregulated free banking allows some addition to the money supply through fractional reserve credit expansion, but this process is restrained by the fear of bankers regarding the threat of bank runs against the gold that supposedly is in reserve against all issues of fiduciary media. (See Chapter 4.)

If the money supply is restricted by free market forces, and if output is increasing through the extension of the division of labor through capital accumulation, then prices of these increasingly plentiful goods should steadily fall. Sellers compete against sellers through price competition in their quest to add to gain money: cash holdings and bank balances. If there were a free market in money, there would be falling prices. Supply would equal demand at prices steadily approaching zero as a limit.

Mises opposed all attempts by the government or the central bank to stabilize prices. There is no way to stabilize prices in a changing world. At best, monetary intervention allows the interventionists to target a particular index number, and then try to keep it stable retroactively, as an echo of today's monetary policy. This leads to the involuntary redistribution of wealth because of the non-neutrality of money. It also leads to the boom-bust business cycle. (See Chapter 5.)

With all of this in mind, let us once again consider the legitimacy of this policy goal:

> There is nothing more important that the government can provide individual producers than a reliable standard of value, a unit of account that retains its constancy as a measuring device.

It should be clear by now that this policy is not based on Misesian economics. Mises did not recommend government monetary policy. He recommended *anti-government monetary policy*. "The first aim of monetary policy must be to prevent governments from embarking on inflation and from creating conditions which encourage credit expansion on the part of banks. But this program is very different from the confused and self-contradictory program of stabilizing purchasing power" (*Human Action*, p. 225).

If the civil government is not supposed to attempt to produce money with stable purchasing power, what of government-licensed banks? I deal with this question in Chapter 4.

4

FRACTIONAL RESERVE BANKING

Fractional reserve banking under a gold standard, as Mises defined it, is a system of lending wherein a bank issues receipts for money metals supposedly held in reserve, which it does not have in reserve. It therefore issues promises to pay, which are legal liabilities for the bank, yet the bank cannot redeem all of these liabilities on demand. Mises called this form of money *credit money or fiduciary media*.

FRACTIONAL RESERVES WITH GOLD

The familiar story of how fractional reserve banking began may be mythical historically, but it does accurately describe the process.

A goldsmith accepts gold bullion as a deposit from a gold owner who wants to have the goldsmith fashion the gold into something lovely. The goldsmith issues a receipt for this specific quantity and fineness of gold. The recipient then finds that he can buy things with the receipt, as if it were gold. The receipt is "as good as gold."

Next, the goldsmith discovers something wonderful for him. He can issue receipts for gold for which there is no gold in reserve. These receipts circulate as if they were 100 percent reserve receipts. They are "as good as what is as good as gold." He can spend them into circulation. Better yet, he can loan them into circulation and receive interest. The new money is cheaper to produce than mining the gold that each receipt promises to pay. The restriction of the money supply that is imposed by the cost of mining is now removed. This is supposedly the origin of fractional reserve banking.

After 1500, yes. Not in the medieval era, I think. I cannot imagine anyone with gold in the late middle ages who would trust a goldsmith with his gold for more than a few days. I also cannot imagine why he would want to spend the receipt. After all, the gold is being hammered into something of beauty. It is becoming more valuable.

There is no doubt that goldsmiths in early modern times did begin to take on the function of banks. At some point, goldsmith-bankers did begin to lend receipts to gold that were not 100 percent backed by gold. They did begin to collect interest payments from borrowers who believed that there was enough gold in reserve to pay off receipts under normal circumstances. Banking in Spain during the sixteenth century adopted fractional reserves, and a series of banking house bankruptcies in second half of the century proved it. The Emperor, Charles V, had legalized the system. As usual, the State authorized the practice of fractional reserve banking as a means of financing itself. It wanted a ready market for its debt.

In a world where all of the receipts for gold that are backed 100 percent by gold (money-certificates) look identical to receipts for gold that are not backed by gold (fiduciary media), the issuing bank faces an opportunity and a threat. The opportunity is to receive something (interest payments) for practically nothing (unbacked receipts for gold). The threat is that word may get out that the bank has issued more receipts for gold than there is gold in reserve, which everyone pretty well knows, especially rival bankers. Then there could be a run on the bank. Bankers who get greedy and issue too many receipts can get caught short. Those people who hold receipts may come down and demand payment of their gold. The gold is not the bank's gold. It is a liability to the bank. The bank has assets to offset the liabilities: credit issued to borrowers. But the receipt-holders are lining up now, and the borrowers do not have to pay until the debts come due, one by one. The bank is "borrowed short" and "lent long." The squeeze is on. The banker then has to go into his Jimmy Stewart routine from *It's a Wonderful Life*, or else face bankruptcy. Not every banker can get Donna Reed to come in and help with the performance.

Everything in bank legislation is tied to one of two goals: preventing bank runs or bailing out bankrupt banks before the panic spreads to other banks. That is, everything in banking legislation is geared to the systematic violation of contracts, either before the bank run or after it begins.

The gold standard for centuries kept fractional reserve banking in golden chains. For over a century—indeed, ever since the creation of the privately owned (until 1946) Bank of England in 1694—central bank policy and government policy have combined to extract physical gold from the owners and transfer it to members of a cartel: bankers. The policy has worked, decade after decade. First, the gold is exchanged for receipts, which are convenient. More receipts are issued than there is gold in reserve. Then, when the bank run begins—always at the outbreak of a major war—the government passes legislation allowing banks to refuse payment of gold during the national emergency.

Every currency devaluation should be understood as the breaking of contract, Mises argued: a violation of contract. He wrote in *Theory of Money and Credit*:

> Credit money has always originated in a suspension of the convertibility into cash of Treasury notes or banknotes (sometimes the suspension was even extended to token coins or to bank deposits) that were previously convertible at any time on the demand of the bearer and were already in circulation. Now whether the original obligation of immediate conversion was

> expressly laid down by the law or merely founded on custom, the suspension of conversion has always taken on the appearance of a breach of the law that could perhaps be excused, but not justified; for the coins or notes that became credit money through the suspension of cash payment could never have been put into circulation otherwise than as money substitutes, as secure claims to a sum of commodity money payable on demand. Consequently, the suspension of immediate convertibility has always been decreed as a merely temporary measure, and a prospect held out of its future rescission. But if credit money is thought of only as a promise to pay, "devaluation" cannot be regarded as anything but a breach of the law, or as meaning anything less than national bankruptcy (p. 233).

Because devaluation is theft by the government, or by its chartered central bank, no one ever gets prosecuted. After World War I, European central bankers persuaded their governments to allow them to keep the stolen gold. Commercial banks were not declared bankrupt by the State for having refused to redeem the receipts, with the owners' gold being returned to them on a pro-rata basis, as would take place in any normal bankruptcy procedure. Instead, the nationally organized gold thieves who had broken their contracts were allowed to keep the stolen goods at cartel headquarters: the national central bank.

The major national exception to this post-World War I central bank strategy of gold collection was the United States. Here, the public had not been persuaded to exchange all of their gold coins for bank receipts. So, in 1933, Franklin Roosevelt unconstitutionally confiscated Americans' gold that was still outside the banks. By unilateral executive order, he made it illegal for American citizens to own any gold coins that had no numismatic value. The government paid the owners $20.67 per ounce. Once the gold was in the possession of the Treasury, Roosevelt officially hiked the price to $35 on January

31, 1934. The Fed then bought the gold from the Treasury by creating new money. This newly issued money was then spent into circulation by the Treasury. The Fed now holds the gold—demonetized—as part of the monetary base.

So, worldwide, governments and central banks steadily removed gold coins from the economy, thereby demonetizing gold. It was the most successful systematic theft operation in human history. It was all done officially. It was all done with paper IOU's to gold that were revoked by sovereign governments, which in turn chose not to be sued by their victims. The public now is unfamiliar with gold coins as a medium of exchange. That was the whole point. The central banks now answer only to bond traders and investors—a narrow market compared to gold coin holders in 1790 or 1890.

This is what every government-operated gold standard has come to. When holders of receipts for gold could sue private local banks that refused to honor those receipts, the gold standard restrained the fractionally reserved commercial banks' proclivity to inflate. When, after World War I, commercial banks and central banks colluded with national governments to allow the banking system to default, and then pass the loot on to the central banks, the gold standard ended. The gold standard was nationalized by governments, then abolished. The central banks thereby demonetized gold, so that they could more efficiently monetize government debt. That was fine with all national governments, whose leaders always want ready markets for the State's debt. This has been the evolution of central banking from 1694 until today.

FRACTIONAL RESERVES WITHOUT GOLD

Commercial banks are still fractionally reserved, but gold is not related to bank accounts any longer. How does the system work today?

A potential depositor goes down to his bank and sees what savings plans are available. He is told that he can make a deposit and get paid interest on it, but withdraw his money at any time. He can have his cake and eat it, too.

The warning bells should go off in the depositor's head, but bankers have done everything possible to keep warning bells from going off. The depositor should ask: "How can the borrower of my money be able to return the money—my money—on the day that I want it back?" He doesn't ask, but he should. The new-accounts lady's misleading but correct answer is: "We keep money in reserve."

More bells. "But how can you make a profit if all of the money we depositors deposit is kept in reserve?" Here, the nicely dressed, low-paid woman sends you to the Assistant Manager. You repeat the question. Her answer is straightforward: "We don't keep all of the money on reserve. We keep 3 percent of it on reserve. We send it to the regional Federal Reserve Bank. We lend out the rest."

More warning bells. "But what if we depositors want to withdraw a total of 4 percent of our money?" Answer: "We would borrow the extra 1 percent from another bank. This is called the federal funds rate." "Why is it called that?" "Because it sounds like the federal government is in on the deal to make it safer." "You mean like the Federal Deposit Insurance Corporation?" "Oh, no; that outfit really is a government organization. It guarantees everyone's accounts up to $100,000." "Really? How much does that organization keep in reserve? "About $1.30 cents per $100 in deposits." "And what does it invest the reserve money in? "U.S. Government debt." "So, if there were a run on all of the banks, where would the government get the money to redeem these debts?" "By selling new debts to the Federal Reserve System." "Where would that organization get the money?" "From its computer. That's where all of the American banking system's money originates. 'The bucks start there,' as we say."

Bells, bells bells: "But if you keep only 3 percent on reserve, and you lend 97 percent, where does the money go when the borrower spends it?" "Into the bank of the person who sells something to the borrower." "What happens to the money that he deposits?" "His bank sets 3 percent aside and lends out 97 percent." "Then what?" "It just keeps rolling along, multiplying as it goes." "How much money does the system create on the basis of the initial issue of money from the Federal Reserve System's computer?" "It's 100 divided by 3, or about 33 to one. Of course, the reserve ratio is higher on large deposits." "But isn't this inflationary, with all that money coming out of the system?" "Only if you define inflation as an increase in the money supply, and only weirdo economists do that anymore."

The initial injection of money comes when a central bank buys an interest-bearing asset that is legal for it to use in its reserves. Legally, the Federal Reserve System can buy an IOU from any entity, but it usually buys U.S. government debt. By creating the money to buy the IOU, the Fed injects original money into the economy, and the fractional reserve process begins the money multiplication process.

Mises was hostile to fractional reserve banking because of its low cost for increasing the money supply—lower than the cost of mining precious metals. This was the same objection that he brought against State-issued money, which I covered in Chapter 2.

SOMETHING FOR NOTHING . . . NOT!

If the borrower wants to borrow money in a non-fractional reserve banking system, a depositor must sacrifice the use of his money—and therefore the goods that his money would otherwise buy—until the repayment date. In a fractional reserve system, he does not sacrifice. He can withdraw his money at any time.

The bank account depositor in a non-fiduciary, 100 percent reserves bank transaction surrenders the use of his money for the duration of the loan: a specified period. He sacrifices his future decision-making ability regarding this money. The borrower gains access to this money, but promises to pay back the loan, plus additional money at the due date. Both the depositor and the borrower suffer a sacrifice in the transaction. The depositor sacrifices the use of the funds; the borrower sacrifices the extra money that must be repaid.

The bank account depositor in a fiduciary transaction is told by the bank that, at any time, he may withdraw the money that he just deposited, either by demanding currency or by writing a check. He has sacrificed no loss of his decision-making ability regarding the future use of this money. The borrower, in contrast, has taken on a legal obligation to repay more money than he received when the note falls due. He has sacrificed his decision-making ability in a way that the depositor has not. This is the heart of the problem, Mises said: the presence or absence of sacrifice. The modern economist would say that the fractional reserve risk-allocating arrangement is asymmetric.

> Credit transactions fall into two groups, the separation of which must form the starting point for every theory of credit and especially for every investigation into the connection between money and credit and into the influence of credit on the money prices of goods. On the one hand are those credit transactions which are characterized by the fact that they impose a sacrifice on that party who performs his part of the bargain before the other does—the forgoing of immediate power of disposal over the exchanged good, or, if this version is preferred, the forgoing of power of disposal over the surrendered good until the receipt of that for which it is exchanged. This sacrifice is balanced by a corresponding gain on the part of the other party to the contract—the advantage of obtaining earlier disposal over the good acquired in exchange, or, what is the same thing, of not having to fulfill his part of the bargain immediately. In their respective valuations both parties

take account of the advantages and disadvantages that arise from the difference between the times at which they have to fulfill the bargain. The exchange ratio embodied in the contract contains an expression of the value of time in the opinions of the individuals concerned.

The second group of credit transactions is characterized by the fact that in them the gain of the party who receives before he pays is balanced by no sacrifice on the part of the other party. Thus the difference in time between fulfillment and counter-fulfillment, which is just as much the essence of this kind of transaction as of the other, has an influence merely on the valuations of the one party, while the other is able to treat it as insignificant. This fact at first seems puzzling, even inexplicable; it constitutes a rock on which many economic theories have come to grief. Nevertheless, the explanation is not very difficult if we take into account the peculiarity of the goods involved in the transaction. In the first kind of credit transactions, what is surrendered consists of money or goods, disposal over which is a source of satisfaction and renunciation of which a source of dissatisfaction. In the credit transactions of the second group, the granter of the credit renounces for the time being the ownership of a sum of money, but this renunciation (given certain assumptions that in this case are justifiable) results for him in no reduction of satisfaction. If a creditor is able to confer a loan by issuing claims which are payable on demand, then the granting of the credit is bound up with no economic sacrifice for him. He could confer credit in this form free of charge, if we disregard the technical costs that may be involved in the issue of notes and the like. Whether he is paid immediately in money or only receives claims at first, which do not fall due until later, remains a matter of indifference to him (pp. 264–65).

Isn't this wonderful? The depositor sacrifices nothing. He gets paid interest, yet he can get back his money at any time.

The borrower gets the use of his money, but he can keep it until the contract comes due. The bank is "borrowed short" (from the depositor) and "lent long" (to the borrower). And not just this bank, but a whole chain of banks. Transaction by transaction, debt by debt, credit by credit, each borrower passes his newly borrowed money to a brand-new depositor-creditor. I recall a bank's ad from my youth: "Watch your money grow!" "Watch the economy's money grow!" is even more informative, but banks do not publicize this sort of educational endeavor. It is too much like Deep Throat's advice to Bob Woodward regarding the Watergate affair: "Follow the money."

MISES VS. FRACTIONAL RESERVES

Mises grew increasingly hostile to fractional reserve banking as he grew older. His 1951 appendix in *Theory of Money and Credit*, "Monetary Reconstruction," represents his post-World War II, post-Keynesian hostility to monetary inflation. But even in 1924, his hostility was apparent.

His two objections to fiduciary media or credit money issued by a fractionally reserved banking system were the same as his objection to any increase in the money supply: its wealth-redistribution effects over time and its creation of a boom-bust business cycle. With respect to the first negative effect, he wrote: "The cost of creating capital for borrowers of loans granted in fiduciary media is borne by those who are injured by the consequent variation in the objective exchange value of money . . ." (p. 314). Borrowers want capital, but they get money—newly created credit money. More credit money has been issued by the banking system than savers have deposited. Those participants in the economy who suffer losses due to price changes were not parties to the original credit transactions. They are participants in the economy who receive the new money late in the process, after prices have been bid up by the credit money. In a chapter titled, "The Evolution of Fiduciary Media," Mises summarized the process of wealth redistribution.

> The requests made to the banks are requests, not for the transfer of money, but for the transfer of other economic goods. Would-be borrowers are in search of capital, not money. They are in search of capital *in the form of money*, because nothing other than power of disposal over money can offer them the possibility of being able to acquire in the market the real capital which is what they really want. Now the peculiar thing, which has been the source of one of the most difficult puzzles in economics for more than a hundred years, is that the would-be borrower's demand for capital is satisfied by the banks through the issue of money substitutes. It is clear that this can only provide a provisional satisfaction of the demands for capital. The banks cannot evoke capital out of nothing. If the fiduciary media satisfy the desire for capital, that is if they really procure disposition over capital goods for the borrowers, then we must first seek the source from which this supply of capital comes. It will not be particularly difficult to discover it. If the fiduciary media are perfect substitutes for money and do all that money could do, if they add to the social stock of money in the broader sense, then their issue must be accompanied by appropriate effects on the exchange ratio between money and other economic goods. The cost of creating capital for borrowers of loans granted in fiduciary media is borne by those who are injured by the consequent variation in the objective exchange value of money; but the profit of the whole transaction goes not only to the borrowers, but also to those who issue the fiduciary media, although these admittedly have sometimes to share their gains with other economic agents, as when they hold interest-bearing deposits, or the State shares in their profits (p. 314).

He favored a privately operated gold standard as a way to hamper the State in its expansion of fiat money (p. 416).

In a chapter in the 1951 appendix's essay, "The Principle of Sound Money," he applied this logic to credit money created by fractional reserve banking.

> What all the enemies of the gold standard spurn as its main vice is precisely the same thing that in the eyes of the advocates of the gold standard is its main virtue, namely, its incompatibility with a policy of credit expansion. The nucleus of all the effusions of the anti-gold authors and politicians is the expansionist fallacy (p. 421).

THE TWO MAIN FUNCTIONS OF BANKING

Mises began a detailed discussion of fractional reserve banking in Part III, Chapter I of *The Theory of Money and Credit*. He pointed to banking's two analytically separate functions: (1) serving as the intermediary between lenders and borrowers; (2) granting credit through the issuing of unbacked credit money, what he called fiduciary media. He insisted that these two aspects of banking must be discussed separately.

> The business of banking falls into two distinct branches: the negotiation of credit through the loan of other people's money and the granting of credit through the issue of fiduciary media, that is, notes and bank balances that are not covered by money. Both branches of business have always been closely connected. They have grown up on a common historical soil, and nowadays are still often carried on together by the same firm. This connection cannot be ascribed to merely external and accidental factors; it is founded on the peculiar nature of fiduciary media, and on the historical development of the business of banking. Nevertheless, the two kinds of activity must be kept strictly apart in economic theory; for only by considering each of them separately is it possible to understand their nature and functions. The unsatisfactory results of previous investigations

> into the theory of banking are primarily attributable to inadequate consideration of the fundamental difference between them (p. 261).

Mises's warning should be taken seriously by his disciples. He warned that previous investigations were unsatisfactory because they confused these two analytically and economically separate economic functions. Therefore, anyone who defends fractional reserve banking because it serves a legitimate function by bringing together borrowers and lenders has confused the two separate functions of fractional reserve banking. Non-fractional reserve banking offers the service of bringing together lenders and borrowers. Mises's objection to fractional reserve banking had nothing to do with banking's function as an intermediary.

Banks serve as intermediaries between lenders who are willing to forego the use of money, meaning everything that this money can buy, for a period of time. They do this in exchange for a promise of a future payment of even greater quantity of money. Put differently, lenders exchange their control over present goods for the promise of future goods. Borrowers gain access to present money (goods) in exchange for future money (goods).

In an exchange apart from fiduciary media, no money is created by this exchange. Money is transferred from lender to borrower; it is not created. This is not true in the case of fiduciary media, meaning bank-created credit money. Because of the fractional reserve process, new money does come into existence.

UNREDEEMED RECEIPTS

This leads to Mises's distinction between consumer goods and money. Money is not a consumer good. It is not desired for its own sake (except, I suppose, by misers). This is why fiduciary media—receipts for money that are not backed by money—can persist in exchange without many demands by receipt-holders to exchange the receipts for goods, whereas claims to consumer goods would be redeemed. Mises used the example of bread. "You can't eat gold," we are told. Quite true, Mises understood. Therein lies the difference in the way that receipts are treated by receipt-holders. He used the examples of receipts for bread and receipts for gold.

> Anyone who wishes to acquire bread can achieve his aim by obtaining in the first place a mature and secure claim to bread. If he only wishes to acquire the bread in order to give it up again in exchange for something else, he can give this claim up instead and is not obliged to liquidate it. But if he wishes to consume the bread, then he has no alternative but to procure it by liquidation of the claim. With the exception of money, all the economic goods that enter into the process of exchange necessarily reach an individual who wishes to consume them; all claims which embody a right to the receipt of such goods will therefore sooner or later have to be realized. A person who takes upon himself the obligation to deliver on demand a particular individual good, or a particular quantity of fungible goods (with the exception of money), must reckon with the fact that he will be held to its fulfillment, and probably in a very short time. Therefore he dare not promise more than he can be constantly ready to perform. A person who has a thousand loaves of bread at his immediate disposal will not dare to issue more than a thousand tickets each of which gives its holder the right to demand at any time the delivery of a loaf of bread. It is otherwise with money. Since nobody wants money except in order to get rid of it again, since it never finds a consumer except on ceasing to be a common medium of exchange, it is quite possible for claims to be employed in its stead, embodying a right to the receipt on demand of a certain sum of money and unimpugnable both as to their convertibility in general and as to whether they really would be converted on the

> demand of the holder; and it is quite possible for these claims to pass from hand to hand without any attempt being made to enforce the right that they embody. The obligee can expect that these claims will remain in circulation for so long as their holders do not lose confidence in their prompt convertibility or transfer them to persons who have not this confidence. He is therefore in a position to undertake greater obligations than he would ever be able to fulfill; it is enough if he takes sufficient precautions to ensure his ability to satisfy promptly that proportion of the claims that is actually enforced against him (pp. 266–67).

So, the total money supply increases as credit money spreads through the fractional reserve banking system, multiplying inversely in terms of the percentage of the reserve. The introduction of new money transfers wealth to early receivers of the new money, at the expense of late users. It also creates an economic boom that will turn into an economic crisis—recession—when the economy adjusts to the new supply of money. (This is Mises's monetary theory of the business cycle, which I cover in Chapter 5.)

In the section, "The Case Against the Issue of Fiduciary Media," Mises said that all banking functions that today are paid for by the profits generated from interest earned on the issue of bank credit money would have to be paid for in a banking system without fractional reserves. In short, there are no free lunches. Making individuals pay for services rendered to them would not destroy banking, he said. "It is clear that prohibition of fiduciary media would by no means imply a death sentence for the banking system, as is sometimes asserted. The banks would still retain the business of negotiating credit, of borrowing for the purpose of lending" (p. 325).

The implication is clear: fractional reserve banking subsidizes users of traditional banking services by transferring wealth to them—wealth that is extracted involuntarily from the victims of credit expansion and the resulting price inflation. It is also paid for by victims of the resulting boom-bust cycle.

FREE BANKING

What should be done to reduce the inflation caused by fractional reserves? Mises took a strictly free-market approach: remove all government protection against bank runs. It should defend the right of contract. The government should favor no bank, charter no bank, license no bank, and regulate no bank. The government should get out of the credit-money subsidy business.

Mises presented a theory of privileged banks and less privileged banks. The State grants protection, and therefore reputation, to certain banks, usually one bank: the central bank.

> Furthermore, within individual countries it is usually possible to distinguish two categories of credit banks. On the one hand there is a privileged bank, which possesses a monopoly or almost a monopoly of the note issue, and whose antiquity and financial resources, and still more its extraordinary reputation throughout the whole country, give it a unique position. And on the other hand there is a series of rival banks, which have not the right of issue and which, however great their reputation and the confidence in their solvency, are unable to compete in the capacity for circulation of their money substitutes with the privileged bank, behind which stands the state with all its authority (p. 326) . . .
>
> It has already been mentioned that in most States two categories of banks exist, as far as the public confidence they enjoy is concerned. The central bank-of-issue, which is usually the only bank with the right to issue notes, occupies an exceptional position, owing to its partial or entire administration by the State and the strict control to which all its activities are subjected. It enjoys a greater reputation than the other credit-issuing

> banks, which have not such a simple type of business to carry on, which often risk more for the sake of profit than they can be responsible for, and which, at least in some States, carry on a series of additional enterprises, the business of company formation for example, besides their banking activities proper, the negotiation of credit and the granting of credit through the issue of fiduciary media. These banks of the second order may under certain circumstances lose the confidence of the public without the position of the central bank being shaken. In this case they are able to maintain themselves in a state of liquidity by securing credit from the central bank on their own behalf (as indeed they also do in other cases when their resources are exhausted) and so being enabled to meet their obligations punctually and in full (p. 333).

Mises did not pursue in his early book the implications of this grant of monopoly privilege on the issuing of fiduciary media. This was a weakness of his earlier writings. In *Human Action*, he rectified the earlier omission.

First, he dealt with traditional suggestions of the need for legislated restrictions on the amount of bank notes. This suggestion as a result of State grants of privilege to banks, which reduced the threat of bank runs.

> It must be emphasized that the problem of legal restrictions upon the issuance of fiduciary media could emerge only because governments had granted special privileges to one or several banks and had thus prevented the free evolution of banking. If the governments had never interfered for the benefit of special banks, if they had never released some banks from the obligation, incumbent upon all individuals and firms in the market economy, to settle their liabilities in full compliance with the terms of the contract, no bank problem would have come into being. The limits which are drawn to credit expansion would have worked effectively. Considerations of its own solvency would have forced

> every bank to cautious restraint in issuing fiduciary media (pp. 437–38).

This policy of special privilege was deliberate, Mises said. "The attitudes of European governments with regard to banking were from the beginning insincere and mendacious. . . . The governments wanted inflation and credit expansion, they wanted booms and easy money" (p. 438).

> It is a fable that governments interfered with banking in order to restrict the issue of fiduciary media and to prevent credit expansion. The idea that guided governments was, on the contrary, the lust for inflation and credit expansion. They privileged banks because they wanted to widen the limits that the unhampered market draws to credit expansion or because they were eager to open the treasury a source of revenue. For the most part both of these considerations motivated the authorities. . . . The establishment of free banking was never seriously considered because it would have been too efficient in restricting credit expansion (p. 438).

Second, he did not call for State regulation over banking. "What is needed to prevent any further credit expansion is to place the banking business under the general rules of commercial and civil laws compelling every individual and firm to fulfill all obligations in full compliance with the terms of the contract" (p. 440). A government can pass a law to restrict the issue of fiduciary media, but this is no better than a statement of good intentions by the government. Then will come some emergency, and "they will always be ready to call their impasse an emergency" (p. 440).

Third, what about a banking cartel? Couldn't banks collude to enable members to issue unlimited quantities of unbacked money? The suggestion is "preposterous," Mises said. "As long as the public is not, by government interference, deprived of the right of withdrawing its deposits, no bank can risk its own good will by collusion with banks whose good will is not so high as its own. One must not forget that every bank issuing fiduciary media is in a rather precarious position. Its most valuable asset is its reputation. It must go bankrupt as soon as doubts arise concerning its perfect trustworthiness and solvency. It would be suicidal for a bank of good standing to link its name with that of other banks with a poorer reputation" (p. 444).

Fourth, what the banking system needs to keep it from expanding fiduciary media is the threat of bank runs by depositors. This will keep banks in line: the threat of bankruptcy. "If the government interferes by freeing the bank from the obligation of redeeming its banknotes and of paying back the deposits in compliance with the terms of the contract, the fiduciary media become either credit money or fiat money. The suspension of specie [gold coin] payments entirely changes the state of affairs" (p. 436).

MISES VS. CENTRAL BANKING

Commercial banking's potential for expanding fiduciary media is minimal compared to central banking, which is protected by government. By 1951, Mises understood that, despite the private ownership of the central banks, governments had created them and had always protected them from bank runs. There has been a joint effort by governments and their monopolistic central banks to destroy free market money. Mises minced no words in his chapter, "The Return to Sound Money," in *The Theory of Money and Credit*.

> The destruction of the monetary order was the result of deliberate actions on the part of various governments. The government-controlled central banks and, in the United States, the government-controlled Federal Reserve System were the instruments applied in this process of disorganization and demolition. Yet without exception all drafts for an improvement of currency

> systems assign to the governments unrestricted supremacy in matters of currency and design fantastic images of super-privileged super-banks. Even the manifest futility of the International Monetary Fund does not deter authors from indulging in dreams about a world bank fertilizing mankind with floods of cheap credit. The inanity of all these plans is not accidental. It is the logical outcome of the social philosophy of their authors (p. 435).

At least he did not refer to the insanity of these plans. Those plans were not insane. They were calculated to expand the supply of unbacked credit money. The result, he predicted in 1912, will be the eventual destruction of money. In a profound prediction made in the first edition of *Theory of Money and Credit*, and reprinted verbatim in the 1924 edition, Mises identified the final goal of all central banking: *the creation of a single world bank*. The goal of the central bankers is the unrestricted issue of unbacked credit money (whose borrowers must pay interest to the issuers).

> 'It would be a mistake to assume that the modern organization of exchange is bound to continue to exist. It carries within itself the germ of its own destruction; the development of the fiduciary medium must necessarily lead to its breakdown. Once common principles for their circulation-credit policy are agreed to by the different credit-issuing banks, or once the multiplicity of credit-issuing banks is replaced by a single World Bank, there will no longer be any limit to the issue of fiduciary media. At first, it will be possible to increase the issue of fiduciary media only until the objective exchange value of money is depressed to the level determined by the other possible uses of the monetary metal. But in the case of fiat money and credit money there is no such limit, and even in the case of commodity money it cannot prove impassable. For once the employment of money substitutes has superseded the employment of money for actual employment in exchange transactions

> mediated by money, and we are by no means very far from this state of affairs, the moment the limit was passed the obligation to redeem the money substitutes would be removed and so the transition to bank-credit money would easily be completed. Then the only limit to the issue would be constituted by the technical costs of the banking business. In any case, long before these limits are reached, the consequences of the increase in the issue of fiduciary media will make themselves felt acutely' (p. 409).

A central bank is a threat to economic liberty. It is also superfluous to the operation of the international gold standard. "The international gold standard works without any action on the part of governments. It is effective real cooperation of all members of the world-embracing market community. . . . What governments call international monetary cooperation is concerted action for the sake of credit expansion" (*Human Action*, p. 473).

I am aware of only one instance in his entire career that he admitted to having made an intellectual error. This was in regard to the creation by the major central banks of a counterfeit gold standard system known as the gold-exchange standard. This system was ratified by international agreement by the Genoa Accords of 1922. It was re-ratified in 1944 by what is known as the Bretton Woods agreement, which created the International Monetary Fund.

The gold exchange standard substituted government debt for gold. Instead of holding gold coins or gold bullion in reserve against the issue of central bank-issued money, central banks held interest-bearing debt certificates issued by a government whose central bank promised to pay other central banks—but not private citizens—a specified amount of gold per unit of the nation's national currency unit. Central banks could then convert a non-interest-paying asset—gold—into an interest-paying asset: a foreign government's bond. In 1922, the favored nations were Great Britain and the United States. In 1944, the only nation was the United States. This system "economized" on the use of gold as a currency reserve. It was an important step in the de-monetization of gold.

Mises faintly praised this arrangement in 1924 in his chapter, "Problems of Credit Policy." This was the final chapter in the 1924 edition of the book. The 1951 appendixes came later. This section was in part prophetic and in part naive.

> Yet the gold-standard system was already undermined before the war. The first step was the abolition of the physical use of gold in individual payments and the accumulation of the stocks of gold in the vaults of the great banks-of-issue. The next step was the adoption of the practice by a series of states of holding the gold reserves of the central banks-of-issue (or the redemption funds that took their place), not in actual gold, but in various sorts of foreign claims to gold. Thus it came about that the greater part of the stock of gold that was used for monetary purposes was gradually accumulated in a few large banks-of-issue; and so these banks became the central reserve banks of the world, as previously the central banks-of-issue had become central reserve banks for individual countries. The war did not create this development; it merely hastened it a little. Neither has the development yet reached the stage when all the newly produced gold that is not absorbed into industrial use flows to a single center. The Bank of England and the central banks-of-issue of some other states still control large stocks of gold; there are still several of them that take up part of the annual output of gold. Yet fluctuations in the price of gold are nowadays essentially dependent on the policy followed by the Federal Reserve Board. If the United States did not absorb gold to the extent to which it does, the price of gold would fall and the gold prices of commodities would rise. Since, so long as the dollar represents a fixed quantity of gold, the United States admits the surplus gold and surrenders commodities for gold to an unlimited extent, a rapid

fall in the value of gold has hitherto been avoided. But this policy of the United States, which involves considerable sacrifices, might one day be changed. Variations in the price of gold would then occur and this would be bound to give rise in other gold countries to the question whether it would not be better in order to avoid further rises in prices to dissociate the currency standard from gold. Just as Sweden attempted for a time to raise the krone above its old gold parity by closing the mint time gold, so other countries that are now still on the gold standard or intend to return to it might act similarly. This would mean a further drop in the price of gold and a further reduction of the usefulness of gold for monetary purposes. If we disregard the Asiatic demand for money, we might even now without undue exaggeration say that gold has ceased to be a commodity the fluctuations in the price of which are independent of government influence. Fluctuations in the price of gold are nowadays substantially dependent on the behavior of *one* government, viz. that of the United States of America (pp. 391–92). . . .

All that could not have been foreseen in this result of a long process of development is the circumstance that the fluctuations in the price of gold should have become dependent upon the policy of one government only. That the United States should have achieved such an economic predominance over other countries as it now has, and that it alone of all the countries of great economic importance should have retained the gold standard while the others (England, France, Germany, Russia, and the rest) have at least temporarily abandoned it that is a consequence of what took place during the war. Yet the matter would not be essentially different if the price of gold was dependent not on the policy of the United States alone, but on those of four or five other governments as well. Those protagonists of the gold-exchange standard who have recommended it as a general monetary system and not merely as an expedient

> for poor countries, have overlooked this fact. They have not observed that the gold-exchange standard must at last mean depriving gold of that characteristic which is the most important from the point of view of monetary policy—its independence of government influence upon fluctuations in its value. The gold-exchange standard has not been recommended or adopted with the object of dethroning gold. . . . But whatever the motives may have been by which the protagonists of the gold-exchange standard have been led, there can be no doubt concerning the results of its increasing popularity.
>
> If the gold-exchange standard is retained, the question must sooner or later arise as to whether it would not be better to substitute for it a credit-money standard whose fluctuations were more susceptible to control than those of gold. For if fluctuations in the price of gold are substantially dependent on political intervention, it is inconceivable why government policy should still be restricted at all and not given a free hand altogether, since the amount of this restriction is not enough to confine arbitrariness in price policy within narrow limits. The cost of additional gold for monetary purposes that is borne by the whole world might well be saved, for it no longer secures the result of making the monetary system independent of government intervention.
>
> If this complete government control is not desired, there remains one alternative only: an attempt must be made to get back from the gold-exchange standard to the actual use of gold again (pp. 392–93).

Mises saw what could come, but he was not that concerned. "Since, so long as the dollar represents a fixed quantity of gold, the United States admits the surplus gold and surrenders commodities for gold to an unlimited extent, a rapid fall in the value of gold has hitherto been avoided. But this policy of the United States, which involves considerable sacrifices, might one day be changed. Variations in the price of gold would then occur and this would be bound to give rise in other gold countries to the question whether it would not be better in order to avoid further rises in prices to dissociate the currency standard from gold." Also, "the gold-exchange standard must at last mean depriving gold of that characteristic which is the most important from the point of view of monetary policy—its independence of government influence upon fluctuations in its value." But then he added, in his naiveté, "The gold-exchange standard has not been recommended or adopted with the object of dethroning gold."

In *Human Action*, he came as close as he ever did to repenting of an intellectual error. "In dealing with the problems of the gold exchange standard all economists—including the author of this book—failed to realize the fact that it places in the hands of governments the power to manipulate their nations' currency easily. Economists blithely assumed that no government of a civilized nation would use the gold exchange standard intentionally as an instrument of inflationary policy" (p. 780). Civil government has acted in a most uncivilized manner through its licensed, privately owned cartels, central banks.

Mises never again made the mistake of trusting any aspect of central banking. By 1949, he had become the most implacable foe of central banking in the economics profession. Only Murray Rothbard has matched him, beginning in 1962 in a chapter appropriately titled, "The Economics of Violent Intervention in the Market" (*Man, Economy, and State*, Chapter 12).

CONCLUSION

Mises's words constitute the best conclusion that I can imagine. First, this passage, taken from the final chapter of the 1924 edition of *The Theory of Money and Credit*. Mises quoted directly from the 1912 edition.

> It has gradually become recognized as a fundamental principle of monetary policy that intervention must

> be avoided as far as possible. Fiduciary media are scarcely different in nature from money; a supply of them affects the market in the same way as a supply of money proper; variations in their quantity influence the objective exchange value of money in just the same way as do variations in the quantity of money proper. Hence, they should logically be subjected to the same principles that have been established with regard to money proper; the same attempts should be made in their case as well to eliminate as far as possible human influence on the exchange ratio between money and other economic goods. The possibility of causing temporary fluctuations in the exchange ratios between goods of higher and of lower orders by the issue of fiduciary media, and the pernicious consequences connected with a divergence between the natural and money rates of interest, are circumstances leading to the same conclusion. Now it is obvious that the only way of eliminating human influence on the credit system is to suppress all further issue of fiduciary media (pp. 407–8).

Second, his recommendation in the 1951 essay, "The Return to Sound Money":

> The first step must be a radical and unconditional abandonment of any further inflation. The total amount of dollar bills, whatever their name or legal characteristic may be, must not be increased by further issuance. No bank must be permitted to expand the total amount of its deposits subject to check or the balance of such deposits of any individual customer, be he a private citizen or the U.S. Treasury, otherwise than by receiving cash deposits in legal-tender banknotes from the public or by receiving a check payable by another domestic bank subject to the same limitations. This means a rigid 100 percent reserve for all future deposits; i.e., all deposits not already in existence on the first day of the reform (p. 448).

In *Human Action*, he called for free banking: the abolition of all government protection of banking. There must be no more grants of privilege or monopoly. There must be the enforcement of contracts.

If Mises was correct, then the unhampered free market will reduce to a minimum the expansion of bank credit money. The State is also removed from the money-production business. This leaves mining as the main source of new money, a source in which costs rise to match revenues, thereby also hampering the expansion of the money supply.

With State-licensed fractional reserve banking, there will be greater instability of money's purchasing power. The system favors inflation. The State literally issues a license to print money, and even worse, create interest-bearing credit that functions as money.

Is the threat merely inflation and its wealth-redistribution effects? Mises said there is another threat: the boom-bust business cycle. I cover this in Chapter 5.

5
THE MONETARY THEORY OF THE BUSINESS CYCLE

Mises regarded his explanation of the business cycle as one of his unique contributions to economic theory. He made more than one: the regression theorem as the theoretical solution to the origin of money, the socialist economic calculation dilemma, and the a priori epistemology for economics. His theory of the monetary origin of the business cycle, he believed in 1931, had been universally accepted. In a 1931 book, *The Causes of the Economic Crisis: An Address*, he went so far as to say: "However, a theory of cyclical fluctuations was finally developed which fulfilled the demands legitimately expected from a scientific solution to the problem. This is the Circulation Credit Theory, usually called the *Monetary Theory of the Trade Cycle*. This theory is generally recognized by science. All cyclical policy measures, which are taken seriously, proceed from the reasoning which lies at the root of this theory" (Mises, *On the Manipulation of Money and Credit* [1978], p. 181). Perhaps he was not overstating the case in 1931, although, academic economists being what they are, I think he was. Today, only Misesians still defend this theory. Among non-Austrian School economists, hardly anyone has heard of it, few of these actually understand it, and nobody believes it.

QUESTIONS RAISED BY RECESSIONS

One of the most familiar criticisms of the free market by its opponents has been the occurrence of economic recessions and occasional economic depressions. Critics point to economic recessions as proof that the unhampered free market does not provide autonomous economic stability. Despite its defenders' claim that the free market social order is self-regulating for the public good, economic recessions have taken place. These recessions are marked by unemployed workers, unemployed resources, rising rates of bankruptcy, general economic contraction, and widespread discontent. This criticism is offered by socialists, mixed-economy interventionists, and monetarists. It is by far the most widely accepted criticism of capitalism. Each group offers a different solution, but all of them are in agreement that civil government must intervene in order to prevent economic recessions from occurring.

Given the existence of recurring recessions, are there modifications of the legal order that will reduce their frequency and intensity, or even eliminate them altogether? If the answer is yes, are these modifications consistent with both the legal assumptions and the economic logic of the free market social order? That is, will these modifications so alter the legal environment that the free market social order will be undermined, or be more likely to be undermined, by the effects that these modifications produce? Will the benefits produced by the reduction or elimination of recessions exceed the costs associated with the changes in the free market social order that the modifications will produce?

There is a narrower technical question that is raised by the existence of economic recessions. If the free market is a system based on competition among entrepreneurs, who are rewarded or punished according to their ability to forecast the economic future and then allocate resources profitably in terms of their plans, why is it that so many of them make the same forecasting error? Why do so many of them fail to forecast the coming economic setback? Why are so few of them able to make plans that will allow them to profit from the recession? In all other conditions, the distribution of profits and losses is allocated by market competition more evenly. In recessions, there are few profits and many losses. Why?

IDENTIFYING THE CAUSE

The question regarding the reasons for the simultaneity of entrepreneurs' errors raises a subordinate question: "What is common to all entrepreneurs in a high division of labor economy?" There is one obvious answer: *a price system that is denominated in money*. Everyone in the economy uses the same monetary system.

Mises began his discussion of the origin of the trade cycle with a discussion of the rate of interest. The interest rate is an aspect of monetary theory, but as he shows, interest is not exclusively an aspect of monetary affairs. Confusion about this has led to erroneous economic policies, such as interest-rate ceilings (usury laws) and false explanations of the business cycle.

In Chapter 19 of *Human Action*, Mises argued that there is always a discount in the price of future goods compared with the price of those same goods in the present. He called this the *originary* rate of interest. It is the product of *time-preference*. Men act in the present; therefore, they prefer goods in the present. Apart from charitable impulses, the only reason why people surrender present goods is in the hope of obtaining a greater value of future goods, other things remaining equal.

This discounting process is applied to all goods, not just money or capital. "If future goods were not bought and sold at a discount as against present goods, the buyer of land would have to pay a price which equals the sum of all future net revenues and which would leave nothing for a current reiterated income" (p. 522). Another example: if a gold mine is expected by all parties to produce one ounce of gold net profit per year for one thousand years, no rational person will pay a thousand ounces of gold, cash up front, to buy it for its gold production. He preferred to keep the gold he already owns. But, at some discounted price, someone will buy it.

The objective discount of future goods against present goods that occurs in the free market is established by the competitive bids of all the sellers of future goods—sellers vs. sellers—and all the competing buyers of future goods: buyers vs. buyers. This discount is called the interest rate.

There are two other factors that make the free market's interest rate. First is the *risk component*. "How likely will the borrower default?" The lender charges an extra percentage to compensate him for this expected risk. Mises discussed this in Chapter 20, Section 2: "The Entrepreneurial Component in the Gross Market Rate of Interest." (Why he used "entrepreneurial" is a mystery. He meant risk, which he, like Frank H. Knight, distinguished from uncertainty. According to both of them, risk can be estimated in advance statistically. Uncertainty cannot. *Human Action*, Chapter 6.) Second, there is the *inflation premium*. "How much should I charge the borrower to compensate me for the expected depreciation of the monetary unit?" He discussed this in Section 3: "The Price Premium as a Component of the Gross Market Rate of Interest." He discussed this in considerable detail in a chapter in *The Theory of Money and Credit*: "The Social Consequences of Variations in the Objective Exchange Value of Money" (pp. 195–203).

The significant component of interest in Mises's theory of the business cycle is the originary rate of interest: the discount of future goods against present goods.

ALLOCATING GOODS THROUGH TIME

We live and consume in the present, but to survive through time, we need additional resources. To secure a supply of future resources, we sacrifice present consumption. An interest rate is the discount that individuals place on the value of future goods compared to present goods. This discount applies to money and everything else. Mises said, "Originary interest is a category of human action. It is operative in any valuation of external things and can never disappear" (*Human Action*, p. 524).

This discount "is a ratio of commodity prices, not a price in itself" (p. 523). "Originary interest is not 'the price paid for the services of capital.' . . . It is, on the contrary, the phenomenon of originary interest that explains why less time-consuming methods of production are resorted to in spite of the fact that more time-consuming methods would render a higher output per unit of input" (p. 523). Interest is not profit. Profit is the difference between the purchase price of a good and its sale price, after having deducted the income that would have been earned by placing the money at interest. Profit originates in the entrepreneur's perception—his guess—that his competitors have underbid the price of some resource, and that future consumers will bid more than his competitors think (p. 532).

If money were neutral and prices were stable—impossible, according to Mises (see Chapter 3)—and if all borrowers always repaid on time and in full (don't lenders wish!), the interest rate would serve only one purpose: to allocate today's resources over time: from now into the indefinite future. Some goods are consumed immediately. Mises called these goods of the first order (p. 93). Production goods that produce first-order goods he calls goods of the second order (p. 94).

A piece of bread is a first-order good. So is a piece of toast. To get a piece of toast, you need a toaster, a second-order good, and electricity, a second-order good (in this example). How much is a toaster worth to you? It is worth what your subjective present valuation of all of pieces of bread it is expected to produce, discounted by your subjective rate of interest, i.e., your discount on all future income.

What does the toaster objectively cost? It initially costs whatever an entrepreneur has estimated that the combined money bids of all potential consumers will be, given the competing offers from other suppliers of goods and services. If he guessed wrong, you may be able to buy it at a discount later.

Will you buy the toaster? Yes, if its objective money price is no higher than your maximum purchase price is, which you established mentally by considering the value to you of other uses for your money in comparison with the value of all those pieces of toast, discounted by your personal rate of interest.

What about the seller who imports toasters? (If you think that most toasters are made in America, you have not been shopping for toasters recently.) Why did he decide to buy all of those toasters in order to make you an offer you obviously can refuse? Because he believed that you and a lot of people just like you would be willing to pay for his toasters at a retail price. He looked at the cost of importing, marketing, and delivering toasters. He estimated the gross revenue from the sale of these toasters. Then he looked at the cost of borrowing money for the time period that concerned him: from his payment to the exporting firm to the sale of the toasters. The market rate of interest was a factor in his decision. Had it been so high that it would have reduced his expected profits on the entire deal, he would not have become a toaster distributor. It was low enough to enable him to make a profit, assuming that he was buying smart and he did not think you and the others would buy even smarter.

As a potential present buyer of a second-order good (toaster), you apply your discount rate to future first-order goods (toast). As a potential seller of future second-order goods (toasters), he has applied the relevant discount rate: the free market's objective rate of interest. Whether you and he can work out an exchange depends on your discount rate (applied to your toast), the market's discount rate (applied to his entrepreneurial plan), and the price of imported toasters vs. the expected retail price.

Oh, yes: one other thing: his competition, meaning everything else that you could use your money to buy.

The entire production process is a series of individual decisions to allocate present goods to their highest uses. Some goods are directly consumed now (bread). Others are directly consumed later (toast). Some are never directly consumed (toasters). They are used to produce goods that are directly consumed (toast). Other goods—goods of a higher order—are used to produce things (steel) that are used to produce second-order goods (toasters).

The same market rate of interest applies to every good during the same time period. If it takes ten years to build a production facility and pay off the loan, then the relevant rate of interest is the ten-year rate. This rate applies equally to every type of production facility that takes ten years to pay off. Whether the facility makes steel or produces chemicals is economically irrelevant to lenders (assuming equal risks of default).

The issue here is goods, not money. "You can't eat gold!" Also, you can't eat Federal Reserve Notes, credit cards, and IOU's from your big-mouth brother-in-law, Harry. But in a money economy, loans are made in terms of money. Therein lies the problem of origin of the trade cycle.

A bank makes loans. A depositor goes to a bank to make a deposit. In a low-risk transaction that does not involve fractional reserves, the depositor would decide what length of time he is willing to forfeit the use of his money. He would then deposit the money. He would not be able to get his money until the due date.

A borrower would also go to the bank. He would borrow the money for that same length of time. The banker would arrange the temporary exchange of funds, making his rate of return on the spread: what he pays the lender vs. what the borrower pays him.

The banker acts as an intermediary. He has information about lending risks. He has information about attracting depositors. He makes his money based on this specialized information.

There is no inflation of the money supply. What the borrower receives, the depositor gives up. The borrower then goes out with his newly borrowed money and bids for goods of a second order (if this is a commercial loan) or goods of the first order (if this is a consumer loan). The depositor cannot bid for any goods. He has forfeited the use of his money.

Under this arrangement, the interest rate allocates goods between first-order uses and higher-order uses in terms of the free market principle, "high bid wins." (To analyze any economic problem, you only need a pair of parrots, one on each shoulder. One is trained to say, "Supply and demand! Supply and demand!" The other says, "High bid wins!" The trick is to listen to them in the correct order, and also to avoid getting dumped on, either by the parrots or economists with their parrots, who are trained to say, "Unfair initial distribution!" and "In the long run, we're all dead!")

DEPOSITS AND LOANS

A depositor makes a deposit. The banker has a new supply of money: a deposit. To make any money on this deal, he has to persuade a borrower to take on a new debt. How does he do this? After all, if the borrower wanted access to the money at today's interest rate, he would have borrowed it this morning. What to do? What to do? Of course! Lower the interest rate. Make him a better deal.

So, bank by bank, deposit by deposit, 97 percent of the total, bankers seek out new borrowers by making them a better deal: a lower interest rate. And borrowers respond to the offer. Every dime gets lent. Every dime has to get lent if the banker wants to make any money on the deal. There are no cookie jars in banks.

Would-be borrowers see lower interest rates available, and they say to themselves, "I can put that money to profitable use. I couldn't at the older, higher rate, but I can now."

At this point, Mises argued, borrowers make errors. They assume, because interest rates are lower, that there has been an increase in demand for future goods. In other words, present-oriented lenders have become less present-oriented. They have decided, "I want additional future goods. I am willing to forfeit the purchase of present consumer goods—sacrifice, in other words—in order to obtain a larger supply of future goods." But the depositors have an ace in the hole: they can change their minds overnight and withdraw their money on demand. They have been promised this by the bankers and the FDIC and Congress and the entire economics profession, except for Austrian School weirdos. They have not agreed contractually to do without consumption goods for the duration of the entire period of the loan. Rather, they have agreed to do without their money until they change their minds. They and the banks agreed to this arrangement "for the duration"—however brief the duration may turn out to be.

The spread of money, you may recall—by now, you had jolly well better recall!—is not neutral. New users get access to it before it loses purchasing power. The cash-induced wealth-redistribution process begins. It shifts demand for from first-order goods to higher-order goods. It subsidizes investment. Mises described this in *Theory of Money and Credit.*

> An increase in the stock of money in the broader sense caused by an issue of fiduciary media means a displacement of the social distribution of property in favor of the issuer. If the fiduciary media are issued by the banks, then this displacement is particularly favorable to the accumulation of capital, for in such a case the issuing body employs the additional wealth that it receives solely for productive purposes, whether directly by initiating and carrying through a process of

> production or indirectly by lending to producers. Thus, as a rule, the fall in the rate of interest in the loan market, which occurs as the most immediate consequence of the increase in the supply of present goods that is due to an issue of fiduciary media, must be in part permanent; that is, it will not be wiped out by the reaction that is afterward caused by the diminution of the property of other persons. There is a high degree of probability that extensive issues of fiduciary media by the banks represent a strong impulse toward the accumulation of capital and have consequently contributed to the fall in the rate of interest.
>
> One thing must be clearly stated at this point: there is no direct arithmetical relationship between an increase or decrease in the issue of fiduciary media on the one hand and the reduction or increase in the rate of interest which this indirectly brings about through its effects on the social distribution of property on the other hand. This would follow merely from the circumstance that there is no direct relationship between the redistribution of property and the differences in the way in which the existing stock of goods in the community is employed. The redistribution of property causes individual economic agents to take different decisions from those they would otherwise have taken. They deal with the goods at their disposal in a different way; they allocate them differently between present (consumptive) employment and future (productive) employment (pp. 349–50).

If the new money goes to producers rather than consumers, there is an increase of demand for, and then production of, investment goods. But investment goods are not liquid assets. They are not the most marketable commodity. In short, they are not money. They are not like a depositor's bank account, withdrawable on demand.

The new money produces a boom in production goods, i.e., a capital equipment boom. Had consumers been willing to forego consumption for a period, such as would be required to issue a 30-year mortgage, this would not be a problem. It would be what consumers really wanted: an increase in future goods in exchange for the consumption and use of present goods. But the banking system is not a 100 percent reserve system in which credit is matched by debt, both in magnitude and duration. It is a fractionally reserved system. It is borrowed short and lent long. It is also inflationary.

So, in terms of what consumers really want, industry is now malinvested. It is loaded up with illiquid goods of a higher order. Consumers were willing to turn over their money to borrowers by way of the banking system, but only given the price conditions that prevailed at the time. These circumstances now begin to change as a result of the new fractional reserve-created money.

Workers who are employed by the capital goods industry now have newly created money to burn. Employment is booming. Their response is predictable: "Let's party!" They start buying consumption goods. The uneven spread of money and prices continues to have its wealth-redistribution effects. The process accelerates.

Other consumers see what is happening to prices. Workers who work in the first-order (consumer) goods industries see demand rising. They also conclude: "Let's party." The new money spreads. As it spreads, prices start rising—prices of consumer goods. Other consumers see this, and they conclude: "If I don't buy now, it will cost me more, later." They start buying.

Back in 1924, let alone 1912, the consumer credit market was a dream of Madison Avenue marketers and General Motors's Alfred Sloan. Europeans knew nothing about such a market. By the time he wrote *Human Action*, Mises should have recognized this new market's effects on his theory of credit money's subsidy of producer goods. He did not mention this, however. There remains therefore a gaping hole in Mises's theory of the trade cycle: consumer credit. Its absence affects the front end of his analysis: where the newly created money gets injected. It also affects the middle of his analysis: the ability of consumers to borrow money to get into the bidding process for consumer goods vs. producer goods. ("High bid wins!") I do not have space here to suggest a modification of his theory, but consumer credit surely makes matters more complex. When a consumer is willing to pay 18 percent or more for a loan, he becomes a strong competitor with a businessman, who knows that 11 percent is the outside limit for his proposed venture. ("High bid wins!")

AFTER THE BOOM, THE BUST

Mises argued that the bust—contraction—is caused by the decisions of consumers to start buying consumer goods earlier than expected by most entrepreneurs. This disrupts the plans of producers, who are caught short with uncompleted projects and rising interest rates. Producers learn painfully that their capital investments had been wrong. The artificially low interest rates created by the expansion of fiduciary money misled them. The consumers really had not become future-oriented. They really were not willing to sacrifice the use of present goods in favor of an increased supply of future goods. The consumers have not changed their minds. Their minds never changed. Depositors were misled by bankers, who offered them an impossible dream: to have their cake (at 3 percent per annum) and eat it too. Now they are eating their cake. As a result, the producers are eating their lunch. In the chapter on "Money, Credit, and Interest," Mises summarized the boom and bust cycle.

(Note: in 1924, Mises called the originary rate of interest the natural rate of interest.)

> The situation is as follows: despite the fact that there has been no increase of intermediate products and there is no possibility of lengthening the average period of production, a rate of interest is established in

the loan market which corresponds to a longer period of production; and so, although it is in the last resort inadmissible and impracticable, a lengthening of the period of production promises for the time to be profitable. But there cannot be the slightest doubt as to where this will lead. A time must necessarily come when the means of subsistence available for consumption are all used up although the capital goods employed in production have not yet been transformed into consumption goods. This time must come all the more quickly inasmuch as the fall in the rate of interest weakens the motive for saving and so slows up the rate of accumulation of capital. The means of subsistence will prove insufficient to maintain the laborers during the whole period of the process of production that has been entered upon. Since production and consumption are continuous, so that every day new processes of production are started upon and others completed, this situation does not imperil human existence by suddenly manifesting itself as a complete lack of consumption goods; it is merely expressed in a reduction of the quantity of goods available for consumption and a consequent restriction of consumption. The market prices of consumption goods rise and those of production goods fall.

That is one of the ways in which the equilibrium of the loan market is reestablished after it has been disturbed by the intervention of the banks. The increased productive activity that sets in when the banks start the policy of granting loans at less than the natural rate of interest at first causes the prices of production goods to rise while the prices of consumption goods, although they rise also, do so only in a moderate degree, namely, only insofar as they are raised by the rise in wages. Thus the tendency toward a fall in the rate of interest on loans that originates in the policy of the banks is at first strengthened. But soon a countermovement sets in: the prices of consumption goods rise, those of production goods fall. That is, the rate of interest on loans rises

> again, it again approaches the natural rate (pp. 362–63).

It gets worse. The interest rate in the initial contraction phase must rise above what it had been prior to the expansion of fiduciary media. One reason is that the price level has risen. "This counter-movement is now strengthened by the fact that the increase of the stock of money in the broader sense that is involved in the increase in the quantity of fiduciary media reduces the objective exchange value of money. Now, as has been shown, so long as this depreciation of money is going on, the rate of interest on loans must rise above the level that would be demanded and paid if the objective exchange value of money remained unaltered" (p. 363). A second reason, which Mises did not mention, is that the risk premium probably rises. More companies are facing bankruptcy. The risk of commercial lending has risen.

> At first the banks may try to oppose these two tendencies that counteract their interest policy by continually reducing the rate of interest charged for loans and forcing fresh quantities of fiduciary media into circulation. But the more they thus increase the stock of money in the broader sense, the more quickly does the value of money fall, and the stronger is its counter-effect on the rate of interest. However much the banks may endeavor to extend their credit circulation, they cannot stop the rise in the rate of interest. Even if they were prepared to go on increasing the quantity of fiduciary media until further increase was no longer possible (whether because the money in use was metallic money and the limit had been reached below which the purchasing power of the money-and-credit unit could not sink without the banks being forced to suspend cash redemption, or whether because the reduction of the interest charged on loans had reached the limit set by the running costs of the banks), they would still be unable to secure the intended result. For such an avalanche of fiduciary media, when its cessation cannot be foreseen,

> must lead to a fall in the objective exchange value of the money-and-credit unit to the panic-like course of which there can be no bounds. Then the rate of interest on loans must also rise in a similar degree and fashion (pp. 363).

Mises insisted that "The essence of the credit-expansion boom is not overinvestment, but investment in the wrong lines, i.e., malinvestment" (*Human Action*, p. 556). The price of all that misallocated capital—illiquid goods of a higher order—must change. The illiquid goods must be either put to lower productive uses or liquidated. How does a businessman get liquid? At a fire sale. Mises described it. "However, raw materials, primary commodities, half-finished manufactures and foodstuffs are not lacking at the turning point at which the upswing turns into depression. On the contrary, the crisis is precisely characterized by the fact that these goods are offered in such quantities as to make their prices drop sharply" (p. 557).

I have used the example of rising prices, but rising prices need not be present in order for Mises's theory to apply. Fractional reserve bank credit is sufficient to cause the boom in malinvested capital. Prices may not rise. They otherwise would have fallen. On this issue, Mises agreed with Murray Rothbard's assessment of the boom of 1926–29: it was not marked by a rise in prices, but the malinvestment of capital did take place. In Regnery's 1966 edition of *Human Action*, Mises wrote: "As a rule the resultant clash of opposite forces was a preponderance of those producing a rise in prices. But there were some exceptional instances too in which the upward movement of prices was only slight. The most remarkable example was provided by the American boom of 1926–29" (p. 561). In a footnote, Mises cited Rothbard's book, *America's Great Depression* (1963). *On the question of the cause of America's great depression, Mises was a Rothbardian.* They both agreed: the cause was monetary policies of the Federal Reserve System—not after the depression began, but before.

The depression is the free market's means of re-pricing goods in terms of the consumers' real priorities between present and future goods. It is not the depression that impoverishes people. It was the boom. "The boom produces impoverishment" (p. 574). By this, he meant "impoverishment as compared with the state of affairs which would have developed in the absence of credit expansion and boom" (p. 562).

Consumers tell producers to pay attention to what consumers really want. They communicate this information with their pocketbooks.

> It is essential to realize that what makes the economic crisis emerge is the democratic process of the market. The consumers disapprove of the employment of the factors of production as effected by the entrepreneurs. They manifest their disapprobation by their conduct in buying and abstention from buying. The entrepreneurs, misled by the illusions of the artificially lowered gross market rate of interest, have failed to invest in those lines in which the most urgent needs of the public would have been satisfied in the best possible way. As soon as the credit expansion comes to an end, these faults become manifest. The attitudes of the consumers force the businessmen to adjust their activities anew to the best possible want-satisfaction (pp. 562–63).

If the public as voters demand that the politicians or central bankers indulge their proclivities for another round of inflation, the boom-bust cycle is extended for another round. So, the real culprits are the voters, who vote to undermine their sovereignty as consumers. In short, said Mises, "the people are incorrigible. After a few years they embark anew upon credit expansion and the old story repeats itself" (p. 576). As Pogo Possum said, "We have met the enemy, and he is us."

CONCLUSION

According to Mises's theory of the business cycle, the free market is not the source of economic contraction, namely, recessions and depressions. The source is the fractional reserve banking system, which is favored by the State. The State licenses a monopolistic central bank—fractionally reserved—which sets monetary policy by buying or selling debt. The commercial banks lend in terms of the reserves created by central bank debt holdings. The central bank and the government protect commercial banks from bank runs by depositors. The State does not enforce the laws of contract as its way to reduce the risk to depositors from default by their over-extended banks. Instead, it protects the banks by creating a special category of contract: the non-enforcement of contract. Then the State increases the profligacy of the bankers by creating a system of government-insured bank deposits. Although Mises did not mention State-provided deposit insurance, he would have seen it for what it is: a device to protect those over-extended banks that default. The State-guaranteed insurance system is a means to persuade the depositors not to worry about unsound banking practices. This reduces the threat of bank runs, i.e., the depositors' means of restricting the banks' issuing of highly leveraged inflationary credit money.

Commercial bank inflation causes the economic boom, which persuades capitalists to misallocate capital, including capital purchased with bank debt. Commercial bank inflation produces this widespread error among entrepreneurs by temporarily lowering the market interest rate below the originary rate, i.e., the rate which allocates the production of present goods vs. future goods in terms of consumer demand for both forms of goods. The discount of future goods against present goods that is established by competing consumers is concealed to entrepreneurs by the interest-rate effects of the newly created fractional reserve—created money that is issued by commercial banks. The temporarily lower rate of interest misinforms capitalist entrepreneurs regarding the investors' true discount of future goods. Capitalist entrepreneurs are misled to believe that savers are more future-oriented than they really are. When the new money raises consumer incomes and then consumer prices, savers reassert their original higher time-preference by buying consumer goods. This disrupts the plans of the now debt-burdened capitalists, who find themselves over-extended. They had thought that consumers wanted to save. Instead, consumers want to spend, and the boom has provided them with new money to spend.

The market-enforced readjustment of prices—consumer goods vs. capital goods—is called a recession. It is the outcome of a prior State-authorized expansion by commercial banks of the supply of credit money. It is the free market's response to a prior interference of the free market's money supply by State-licensed, State-protected fractional reserve banks.

Mises wrote a brief 1936 essay in French. It was translated into English in 1978 and published in a booklet by the Center for Libertarian Studies: *The Austrian Theory of the Trade Cycle and Other Essays*. He concluded:

> Public opinion is perfectly right to see the end of the boom and the crisis as a consequence of the policy of the banks. The banks could undoubtedly have delayed the unfavorable developments for some further time. They could have continued their policy of credit expansion for a while. But—as we have already seen—they could

> not have persisted in it indefinitely. The boom brought about by the banks' policy of extending credit must necessarily end sooner or later. Unless they are willing to let their policy completely destroy the monetary and credit system, the banks themselves must cut it short before the catastrophe occurs. The longer the period of credit expansion and the longer the banks delay in changing their policy, the worse will be the consequences of the malinvestments and the inordinate speculation characterizing the boom; and as a result the longer will be the period of depression and the more uncertain the date of recovery and return to normal economic activity (pp. 5–6).

Mises's theory of the business cycle places secondary responsibility for the boom, with all of its malinvestment, on the profit-seeking bankers who use the fractional reserve banking system to create interest-bearing credit money. His theory places greater responsibility on the politicians. By legalizing special exemptions for bankers with respect to the obligation to honor contracts, the politicians have undermined the free market's early phase negative sanctions against over-extended fractionally reserved banks. Instead, the later-phase sanctions come into play: the bust, unemployment, and the bankruptcy of businesses and the banks that lured them into disaster.

To the extent that a national government adds another layer of protection from free market sanctions in the form of a central bank cartel that has the power to issue money—sometimes called high-powered money, because it serves as legal reserve for the expansion of commercial bank credit—responsibility shifts from commercial bankers to central bankers. Mises was a great opponent of central banks.

Ultimately, citizens are to blame. They think that they can get something for nothing. They think that they can make themselves wealthier by spending newly created credit money. They have two generations of Keynesian economists telling them that they really can do this. They are present-orientated. In Mises's terminology, they have high time-preference. They have a willingness to go into debt at high interest. They place a high discount on future goods. Whenever there is a slowdown in the increase of fractionally reserved credit money, their high time-preference produces a recession. Then consumers, in their legal capacity as voters, tell the politicians to Do Something. The politicians in turn call on the central bank to create more money and thereby lower interest rates, in order to restore the economic boom. The central bank opens up the high-powered money spigot even wider by buying government debt. The Treasury spends the new money into circulation, and the recipients deposit it in their local banks. The commercial banks start lending their newly created credit money to anyone who will take on more debt. The money gets spent by the borrowers. The recipients bid up prices. The central bank then ceases to create new high-powered money, so as not to destroy the currency unit by inflating. Another recession occurs. And the beat goes on. And the beat goes on.

This leaves us with the perennial question: "What is to be done?" I suggest answers in the following Conclusion.

CONCLUSION

Ludwig von Mises made several important contributions to the theory of money: the refutation of any concept of neutral money that somehow does not redistribute income when the money supply changes; the idea of every existing money supply as maximizing benefits to participants in an indirect-exchange economy; changes in the money supply as conferring no identifiable increase in social value; and the monetary theory of the business cycle. In my opinion, these were peripheral to his major contribution to monetary theory. His most important and unique contribution was a single idea, which is denied by all other schools of economic opinion:

> The State's coercive interference in either money or banking, including its licensing of a monopolistic central bank, reduces all men's freedom and most men's wealth.

Mises offered a theory of money and credit that is "market endogenous," i.e., a theory of money that affirms the free market's ability, through men's voluntary transactions, to establish market-clearing prices, day after day, year after year, apart from any government agency's decree. All other schools of monetary thought deny the ability of an autonomous, self-regulating free market to maximize efficiency, freedom, and productivity. Every other school of opinion calls for State intervention into the money supply: always increasing it, never decreasing it. All other schools of thought favor the creation of a central bank, legally independent of the government, yet the offspring of the government, possessing a lawful monopoly over the control of the money supply. *In short, all other schools of economics are statist in their theory of money and credit.*

Mises, by establishing his theory of money on the conceptual foundation of the free market, alone offered a completely free market theory of money and credit. He called on civil governments to enforce banking contracts that establish both money certificates and credit money, just as governments should enforce all other private contracts. Mises offered a theory of money and credit in which civil governments have no monetary policies at all.

A FREEZE ON ADDITIONAL GOVERNMENT MONEY

A free market money system does not exist today. Every national government, through its licensed monopoly, the fractionally reserved central bank, and its licensed oligopolies, fractionally reserved commercial banks, is deeply involved in setting monetary policy. For national governments in general and the U.S. government in particular, Mises had a single policy recommendation: *create no new money*. He made this point in his 1951 essay, "The Return to Sound Money."

> The first step must be a radical and unconditional abandonment of any further inflation. The total amount of dollar bills, whatever their name or legal characteristic may be, must not be increased by further issuance. No bank must be permitted to expand the total amount of its deposits subject to check or the balance of such deposits of any individual customer, be he a private citizen or the U.S. Treasury, otherwise than by receiving cash deposits in legal-tender banknotes from the public or by receiving a check payable by another domestic bank subject to the same limitations. This means a rigid 100 percent reserve for all future deposits; i.e., all deposits not already in existence on the first day of the reform (p. 448).

Where statist money is concerned, Mises had only one suggestion: do not add to the money supply. Enough is enough.

Mises also opposed deflation as a policy, just as he opposed inflation. But, most important and most adamantly, he opposed any further intervention by the State or its central bank to increase the money supply. He wanted government out of the money-creation business. Every anti-inflation policy must begin with the policy-makers' refusal to add to the central bank's monetary base.

This position has a corollary, which Mises stated explicitly: the State and the central bank must not interfere with bank runs. There should be no State intervention of any kind in saving over-extended banks that are being bankrupted by their depositors. It is the State's attempt to undermine contracts that is the root cause of credit-money inflation. No bank should be too small to fail or too big to fail. The threat of bankruptcy must be on the mind of every banker at all times, in order to offset his temptation to issue fiduciary media.

This position leads to a policy conclusion: *The deflation of the money supply is valid if this deflationary process is the result of depositors' withdrawal of their funds and the conversion of these funds into currency, which is not fractionally reserved.* To the degree that the existing money supply is the result of fractional reserve banking, the State and its central bank should accept any deflation that results from the reduction of fractional reserves by the decisions of depositors to exchange deposits for currency and not redeposit their money in another member bank in the fractional reserve banking system. A bank run is the depositors' negative sanction that provides them with their sovereignty over their own property, i.e., their money.

As a defender of the ideal of free banking (see Chapter 5), Mises again and again warned the State not to intervene in banking affairs, except to enforce contracts. The depositors' decision to withdraw their funds by converting their deposits into currency is the essence of the original contract between banks and depositors. So, while Mises was not an advocate of the State's deliberate policy of deflation, he was a strong advocate of the legal right of depositors to withdraw their money out of their banks on demand. The State should not intervene in order to save over-extended commercial banks. But over-extended banks, by becoming insolvent, reduce the supply of credit money. Thus, Mises was not an opponent of deflation in general, for thus would have made him an opponent of depositor-induced deflation. He was an opponent of State-induced deflation. Nowhere in his writings did he recommend that the State or the central bank create new monetary reserves in order to offset a reduction in the money supply caused by depositors' withdrawal of their funds. On the contrary, in "The Return to Sound Money," he told us that what is required is a complete freeze on the central bank's creation of additional money, for any reason.

> Sound money still means today what it meant in the nineteenth century: the gold standard.

The eminence of the gold standard consists in the fact that it makes the determination of the monetary unit's purchasing power independent of the measures of governments. It wrests from the hands of the "economic tsars" their most redoubtable instrument. It makes it impossible for them to inflate. This is why the gold standard is furiously attacked by all those who expect that they will be benefited by bounties from the seemingly inexhaustible government purse.

What is needed first of all is to force the rulers to spend only what, by virtue of duly promulgated laws, they have collected as taxes. Whether governments should borrow from the public at all and, if so, to what extent are questions that are irrelevant to the treatment of monetary problems. The main thing is that the government should no longer be in a position to increase the quantity of money in circulation and the amount of checkbook money not fully—that is, 100 percent—covered by deposits paid in by the public. No backdoor must be left open where inflation can slip in. No emergency can justify a return to inflation. Inflation can provide neither the weapons a nation needs to defend its independence nor the capital goods required for any project. It does not cure unsatisfactory conditions. It merely helps the rulers whose policies brought about the catastrophe to exculpate themselves.

One of the goals of the reform suggested is to explode and to kill forever the superstitious belief that governments and banks have the power to make the nation or individual citizens richer, out of nothing and without making anybody poorer. The short-sighted observer sees only the things the government has accomplished by spending the newly created money. He does not see the things the non-performance of which provided the means for the government's success. He fails to realize that inflation does not create additional goods but merely shifts wealth and income from some groups of

> people to others. He neglects, moreover, to take notice of the secondary effects of inflation: malinvestment and decumulation of capital (pp. 438–39).

Mises suggested a reform: the re-establishment of a traditional, government-guaranteed gold standard. The likelihood of implementing this reform rested on an assumption: "Keynesianism is losing face even at the universities" (p. 439). His timing was way off. Keynesianism had only just begun to exercise control over every area of American economic opinion. When, in the mid-1960s, monetarism visibly raised its anti-gold standard head, the case against the gold standard and in favor of fiat money grew even more academically acceptable. Thus, his statement in 1951 seems utopian today: "The political chances for a return to sound money are slim, but they are certainly better than they have been in any period after 1914" (p. 439).

Mises opposed a State-imposed policy of deflation. To re-establish a traditional gold standard, the national civil government must guarantee to buy and sell gold at an official price. For a national government to re-establish the official price of gold at the price that had prevailed before the expansion of credit money would require a policy of deflation leading to economic contraction. This is what Great Britain had done after the Napoleonic Wars in 1815 and after World War I in 1925. Mises regarded both decisions as unwise (p. 455). So, Mises said, the official price of gold should be restored at something close to the free market price. He said that the Treasury must sell gold at the fixed price for what we call M-1: currency, token coins, and checks drawn upon a member bank (p. 450).

He did not say, but obviously believed, that the monetary reserves of the central bank must not increase as the result of a hike in gold's official price. The official price today is $42.22 per ounce. It was $35 in 1951. He thought that it might have to be raised to somewhere between $36 and $38 (p. 449)—

perhaps 10 percent. If gold's official price were raised to the free market's price today, the Federal Reserve System's Open Market Committee (FOMC) would be required to sell Treasury debt to offset the gold price revision's increase in the monetary base. Alternatively, the Fed's Board of Governors would have to raise the reserve requirements for commercial banks. Either policy would raise interest rates.

The gold reserves of the United States in December, 2001, totalled a little over $11 billion at the official price of $42.22. This would have to be multiplied by about seven, or about $77 billion, an increase of $66 billion. The FOMC would then have to sell $66 billion of Treasury debt. With the adjusted monetary base at about $655 billion, this would be a 10 percent decrease in the monetary base. This would raise short-term interest rates. If the Federal Reserve System then refused to interfere by adding to reserves—which Mises's reform proposal mandated—a deflation of the money supply would take place when bank runs toppled insolvent banks. There would be a recession, or worse.

Mises's proposal was to restore the traditional government-guaranteed gold standard, in which every national government's central bank would still keep on deposit the bulk of the national economy's gold. If the public were to begin to redeem gold, the central bank would then sell Treasury debt, thereby deflating the money supply, thereby raising interest rates, thereby halting the gold outflow. "Keep your money in the bank at high interest rates. Don't withdraw non-interest-paying gold." Deflation with rising interest rates create recessions.

The money-stabilizing strategy of the traditional gold standard always assumed that most people would always leave most of their gold on deposit with the commercial banks (pre-1914) or with the central bank (post-1914). Put another way, the logic of the traditional State-run gold standard assumes that the public must always be kept from reclaiming most of its gold by having banks call in loans, shrink the money supply, and raise interest rates. But there is always the other option for the banks:

default. The political popularity of default eventually wins out over the pain of recession. At that point, advocates of the gold standard are back to square one: blamed for the recession and rejected as obsolete voices of the past. They are dismissed by politicians and economists as barbarous relics.

Leaving gold in the possession of fractional reserve bankers is like issuing a license for them to steal the gold whenever some emergency appears that supposedly justifies the State's suspension of gold convertibility, i.e., another violation of contract. Once people's gold is in the possession of fractional reserve banks, it will not be returned to them. Initially, banks will raise interest rates by reducing credit money in order to persuade depositors not to reclaim their gold. When this fails to persuade them, the banks will steal their gold by defaulting on their contracts to redeem gold on demand, and the State will authorize this. Once a nation's gold supply goes into a fractional reserved banking system, most of it never comes out. This is the golden rule of fractional reserve banking: *Do unto depositors before the depositors do it unto you*. Mises did not formulate this rule; I did. He merely described its operation. I learned how it operates from him.

Mises wrote in 1951: "The Classical or orthodox gold standard alone is a truly effective check on the power of the government to inflate the currency. Without such a check all other constitutional safeguards can be rendered vain" (p. 452). Mises in this passage implicitly accepted the fact that the United States government, through its monopolistic central bank, controlled the money supply in his day. The United States government had confiscated the public's gold in 1933. Mises in 1951 affirmed the classical gold standard as the only way to keep the civil government from inflating the money supply. This does not mean that he believed that only the civil government should control the money supply. He did not believe this. On the contrary, he believed that the free market should be the sole source of money. He defended this position when no other economist was willing to. His followers still are the only economists who defend this proposition. The classical gold standard was his recommended policy for an undesirable condition: control over money by civil government.

The political theory of judicial sovereignty rests on a presupposition: there is no higher earthly court of appeal beyond a sovereign State. This is an updated version of early modern Europe's doctrine of the divine right of kings. This doctrine was popular with King James I. It was rejected by his contemporary, the English constitutional law jurist, Sir Edward Coke ["Cook"]: Petition of Right (1628). The theory of the classical gold standard assumes the legal sovereignty of the State over money. In terms of this theory, there is no judicial authority to preserve the classical gold standard from the government's desire to escape its restrictions. The classical gold standard, by definition, is self-imposed by the civil government. So, when incumbent politicians in search of new money to buy votes tire of this self-imposed limitation, they abandon it. Who can stop them? Not depositors, who are the default's immediate victims. Not voters, who do not understand monetary theory. Not Keynesian or monetarist economists, who hate the gold standard. Not supply-side economists, who are of two opinions during recessions: the need to defend the gold standard and the need for the central bank to create more money, after tax cuts have failed to revive the sagging economy.

By 1949, Mises had no illusions about the honesty of governments or their statutory creations, central banks. In *Human Action*, he wrote derisively of the Bretton Woods gold-exchange standard: "In dealing with the problems of the gold exchange standard all economists—including the author of this book—failed to realize the fact that it places in the hands of governments the power to manipulate their nations' currency easily. Economists blithely assumed that no government of a civilized nation would use the gold exchange standard intentionally as an instrument of inflationary policy" (p. 780).

A gold standard that the public can safely rely on must not have anything to do with a government's guarantee to redeem gold on demand. Such a guarantee is unenforceable in any government court after the government revokes it. Governments eventually cheat on their promise to redeem money-certificates for gold. They either devalue the currency (lower the quantity of gold redeemable per currency unit) or else they default: cease redeeming IOU's for any quantity of gold. There have been no exceptions in history.

The definition of a crazy person is someone who keeps doing something, over and over, even though it fails to achieve his goal. It is time for defenders of sound money to cease being crazy. It is time to stop promoting the traditional gold standard. The traditional gold standard is a game for suckers. The government or its licensed agents announce: "Bring us your gold, and we will store it for you free of charge, and you can get it back at any time at the price at which you sold it us." To which I reply: "There ain't no such thing as a free government-guaranteed gold standard."

How, then, can a nation return to a gold standard that is the product of the free market rather than the State? I offer the following suggestion in the spirit of Mises, though not the letter.

"MR. BERNANKE, TEAR DOWN THESE WALLS!"

In the underground vault at 33 Liberty Street, New York City, the Federal Reserve Bank of New York stores most of the world's gold. This gold belongs to central banks. It used to belong to private citizens. The vault's walls protect the Federal Reserve's gold and foreign central banks' gold from the public. There are walls for the vault at Fort Knox that perform the same restrictive function.

All over the world during the twentieth century, the State, in conjunction with State-created central banks, deliberately stole the public's gold. In Europe, this was done in two steps. At the beginning of World War I, every government passed laws allowing its commercial banks to refuse to redeem gold on demand. (Step one.) Governments thereby escaped a future vote of monetary no confidence by depositors who had unwisely trusted the State to enforce laws of contract. The depositors' IOU's to gold became "IOU-nothings." The national central banks then created additional fiat money and bought the newly confiscated gold. (Step two.) The gold wound up in the vaults of the national central banks or their main fiduciary agents, the Bank of England and the newly created Federal Reserve System.

The Fed's gold, which was bought and paid for with its very own fiat money, along with foreign central banks' gold that is held for safekeeping and convenient inter-bank swapping, has always been stored at the Federal Reserve Bank of New York.

> [Note: the day that this gold begins to be shipped to Basle, Switzerland, to be held for safekeeping by the Bank for International Settlements, is that day that American sovereignty gets unofficially transferred.]

In the United States, the theft was more blatant: in 1933, the government made it illegal for American citizens to own non-numismatic gold coins or non-jewelry gold. The government openly stole the gold from the public, and then sold it to the Federal Reserve System in exchange for the Fed's newly issued money. Then the Treasury spent the newly created money. (See Chapter 4.)

Central banks have demonetized gold by stealing it. This has enabled them to monetize government debt with far less restriction: no threat of any withdrawals of gold by the previous private owners of gold. This demonetization of gold took place three generations ago in Europe, two generations ago in the United States. It is "old news." This happened so long ago that it was never on anyone's radar screen. It happened prior to the invention of radar.

How can the public re-monetize its gold? By demanding the return of the gold. Central banks must be compelled by law to return the stolen goods. The stolen gold surely will not be returned by the thieves voluntarily. (Here, let me imitate a Chicago School economist: "Let us assume that there are two people, a thief and his victim's grandson. The thief has on his side the police, the media, and every economics department on earth, including mine. If transaction costs were zero, the victim's grandson could suggest a mutually beneficial exchange." And so forth.)

I am unaware of any non-Austrian school of economic opinion that has seriously suggested the return of central banks' gold to the public. The operating assumption of all rival schools of monetary opinion is this: "Stealers, keepers; losers, weepers." Also, "Possession is ten-tenths of the law."

This return of the public's gold need not be deflationary. Each government could issue non-interest-bearing, 100-year bonds to its central bank. The bonds should be equal in value to the officially listed value of the central bank's gold supply. In the United States, this would be $42.22 per ounce times the ounces held, or $11 billion. This gold presently earns no interest; therefore, neither should the bonds. The bonds will replace the gold as the central bank's legal reserve for the nation's money supply. No muss, no fuss: call these bonds a gold tranche or whatever fancy-Dan word that economists choose. I would call them Solvency Operating Bonds, or SOB's.

The Treasury Departments of the world would then possess the gold that they sold decades ago to their central banks. But not for long. All of this gold—every ounce—would be sold to the public in the form of coins, preferably one-tenth of a troy ounce of gold, 99.9 percent fine, but with additional copper or some other hardening metal, so that the coins can circulate without much wear. The time limit on the sale of this gold would depend on the output of the mint on a 24 x 6 schedule. (Give them Sundays off.) The government will then use the income generated from the sale of the coins to reduce the government's debt. (This debt-reduction procedure is not necessary to make the transition to a full gold coin standard, but since I'm dreaming of that which is politically remote, why not dream big?)

If the sale of gold is politically unacceptable, then the government can hold a national lottery, with all of the proceeds going to the two dominant political parties, or to whatever other boondoggle is acceptable to Congress. I do not care who gets the lottery money. I care who gets ownership of the gold coins: the public. I think a national lottery would generate more public interest in the coins than a series of auctions. There is already an existing distribution system: local convenience stores. Let local banks get involved, too. "Come one, come all: get your tickets here!"

Call the lottery "Golden Opportunity," or "El Dorado," or "Streets of Gold," or "End of the Rainbow." Call it "Return of Stolen Goods." Whatever some New York ad agency thinks will work, use.

Whether bought from the government or won from the government, the coins will enjoy income-tax-free status for five years. The deal would be this: unless the recipient sells the coins for currency or bank credit money, he can keep them or trade them, income-tax-free, for five years. So can the people who receive them in exchange. Each coin will be income tax-free money for 60 months after the release date of the coin, which will be stamped accordingly.

Want to replace the fiat money standard? Want alternative markets in which gold coins are recognized and sought-after? Just grant income-tax-free status to each coin for five years. The "good" coins—tax-free time remaining—will drive the "bad" coins out of circulation after five years. This is the opposite of Gresham's Law. The "defunct" coins will then be used mainly in what I prefer to call *unofficial markets*, which will have several years to develop.

The reason why the coins should be tenth-ounce coins is simple: no one will want to receive change in paper money, because this change would constitute taxable income: selling for paper money part of the value of a tax-exempt coin. No one will want to receive taxable money for tax-free money. The coins must therefore be small-weight coins.

The governments of the world are not about to give up their control over bank credit money. The world is dependent on the existing structure of credit-money prices. What I am proposing is the creation of a parallel standard. Mises argued that parallel standards for gold and silver existed for millennia. This is what I am proposing: a free market gold coin standard side by side with a fiat money standard for the government's bank money, which we have anyway. All that my proposal would change is this: the return of the stolen gold.

This gold-transfer program would be opposed by "gold bugs," who are invested in gold. The price of gold would fall if all governments started selling all of the gold they have repurchased from the central banks. Gold bugs are like condominium owners in New York City who are opposed to price controls in general, but opposed to the abolition of rent controls in New York City. Such an abolition would produce windfall profits for the owners of rent-controlled buildings, and capital losses for owners of condos. The available supply of condo-competing rental property would increase. There would be fewer cheap middle-class apartments, but the market for condos would go down.

What is good for the world would not be good in the short run for gold bugs, of whom I am chief. That is the price of liberty.

Is my suggested reform politically possible because it is conceptually possible? No. I have described this reform only as an exercise to demonstrate that a top-down, non-deflationary, political reform of the banking system is conceivable. The public might respond favorably to the offer of economic liberty, if given the opportunity. But this opportunity will not be given—surely not by the present system's beneficiaries, central bankers, who long ago established the terms of debate regarding central banking. The debate is this: politically independent national central banks vs. a single politically independent international central bank. Other debaters need not apply.

Nevertheless, there will be a reform, one that undermines central banking.

MARKET-IMPOSED REFORM

The public will at some point break the banks by abandoning today's officially sanctioned money system. The central banks will inflate to keep the inflation-induced economic boom alive. The public, through the free market, will eventually abandon the official money system and substitute an alternative monetary unit on its own authority. Mises spelled this out in 1912: "It would be a mistake to assume that the modern organization of exchange is bound to continue to exist. It carries within itself the germ of its own destruction; the development of the fiduciary medium must necessarily lead to its breakdown" (*TM&C*, p. 409). The defenders of central banking have persuaded the public that the great advantage of central banking is "flexible money." The public is going to get flexible money, good and hard.

The banks' self-destruction could also go the other way: mass deflation. Banks at the end of some future trading day may not be able to clear their accounts with each other because of an unforeseen breakdown in the international payments system. They may cease operating because of what Greenspan has called a cascading chain reaction of cross-defaults.

> To be sure, we should recognize that if we choose to have the advantages of a leveraged system of financial intermediaries, the burden of managing risk in the

> financial system will not lie with the private sector alone. As I noted, with leveraging there will always exist a possibility, however remote, of a chain reaction, a cascading sequence of defaults that will culminate in financial implosion if it proceeds unchecked. Only a central bank, with its unlimited power to create money, can with a high probability thwart such a process before it becomes destructive. Hence, central banks will of necessity be drawn into becoming lenders of last resort. But implicit in the existence of such a role is that there will be some form of allocation between the public and private sectors of the burden of risk, with central banks responsible for managing the most extreme, that is the most systemically sensitive, outcomes. Thus, central banks have been led to provide what essentially amounts to catastrophic financial insurance coverage. Such a public subsidy should be reserved for only the rarest of disasters. If the owners or managers of private financial institutions were to anticipate being propped up frequently by government support, it would only encourage reckless and irresponsible practices. (Speech, "Understanding today's international financial system," May 7, 1998; http://bit.ly/Greenspan1998)

Like a juggler with too many oranges in the air at one time, fractional reserve banking looks impressive for a while. Then it fails, taking the division of labor with it. This is the ultimate price of fractional reserve banking: the *universally unexpected reduction in the division of labor*.

Expect it.

NO OFFICIAL PRICE OF GOLD

Gold does not need an official price because no price needs to be official. An official price is set by government officials. That is the problem with every official price. The great advantage of a free market, gold coin standard is that no government official possesses the legal authority to set an official price for gold.

The classical, government-guaranteed gold standard was never any better than a government's promise to allow the public to redeem gold at an officially fixed price. In every case, governments eventually defaulted.

No defrauded citizen can successfully sue a national government for its having defaulted on its promise to redeem gold at a fixed price, for the courts of the national government regard the national government as legally sovereign, therefore enjoying sovereign immunity from lawsuits that either the politicians or the courts choose not to hear. When an official IOU for gold is issued by a civil government or its licensed agent, the central bank, it is worth the now-used paper that it is printed on. Any value greater than this is the free market's imputed value to the government's promise. In every case, this promise has been broken.

There are a handful of people—only rarely are they academically certified economists—who still call for a restoration of some version of the classical gold standard, or even some version of the central banks' gold-exchange standard. These people are well-intentioned but naive. They look at a system that defaulted in 100 percent of the cases during the twentieth century, yet they still call for its restoration. They honestly expect to gain a permanent monetary system settlement on their terms from the well-organized enemies of every gold standard, whose power and wealth would be restricted by any gold standard. Mises wrote in 1944, "The gold standard did not collapse. The governments destroyed it" (*Omnipotent Government*, p. 251). In the face of this historical reality, today's tiny army of true believers who defend a government-guaranteed gold standard tell us, "Next time, it will be different." These people are slow learners.

National central banks now own the people's gold. They are unlikely to surrender this stolen gold until they have to. This "have to" will be imposed, if at all, by some market crisis, not by conventional, pre-crisis politics. Politically, there will be no change that significantly restricts central banks' power over money until the voting public imposes a change. This will not happen until voters not only understand the logic of the free market gold standard but are also ready to make this reform a single issue in their voting behavior.

Today, there is no understanding of the gold standard, classical or free market, especially among economists. The public has forgotten all about a gold coin standard. People have no awareness that the world's central banks stole their grandparents' and great-grandparents' gold coins. There will be no groundswell of political opinion in favor of a free market gold coin standard until there is an economic crisis that forces a reconsideration of monetary policy on the politicians.

Political economic policy is preceded by economic theory. Today, the anti-gold bias of monetary theorists is overwhelming. Every school of economic opinion except the Austrian School believes that a national government should enforce the decisions of its central bank, which establishes and enforces national monetary policy. The only exceptions to this rule are a few internationalists who believe that a world central bank should establish monetary policy for every nation.

ADVICE TO WOULD-BE REFORMERS

Leonard E. Read, the founder in 1946 of the Foundation for Economic Education, used to say that we should postpone our attempts to implement our grand schemes until we have made major progress in our own personal programs of self-education and self-reform. Our reforms should begin at home. I agree.

I have written this little book on Mises's view of money in order to help readers begin to think about the issue of money—in both senses—and help them begin their own programs of intellectual and financial self-improvement. Mises offered a theory of money that was self-consciously based on a theory of individual decision-making. He offered no grand scheme for political reform. He offered only one policy: *shrink the State.*

Mises presented a comprehensive theory of money which rested on only two legal pillars, both of which have been undermined by modern law: (1) the enforcement of contracts by the civil government; (2) the right of peaceful, non-fraudulent voluntary exchange. His monetary theory was a consistent extension of his theory of the free market. He did not rely on a theory of State regulation of the monetary system, any more than he relied on a theory of State regulation of any other sphere of the economy. He denied the need for such regulation. He showed why such regulation is counter-productive for a society. He recommended only one monetary policy: the State's enforcement of voluntary contracts. That was his recommended economic policy in general. This minimalist theory of civil government makes his theory of money unique in the history of academic economic thought.

Mises's answer to the question, "What kind of money should we have?" was simple: "whatever individuals voluntarily choose to use." He wanted the State to get out of the money business. This included the State's monopolistic agent, the central bank. He offered a comprehensive theory of money that demonstrated that the State does not need to be in the money business in order for a free market social order to prosper. The money system, as is true of the other subdivisions in a free market economy, is part of a self-adjusting, self-correcting system of dual sanctions. These dual sanctions are profit and loss. Money is market-generated. It is also market-regulated. It is a product of consumer sovereignty, not State sovereignty. The State is always an interloper in monetary affairs. The State reduces market freedom and efficiency. The State makes things worse from the point of view of long-term economic stability. So does the State's now-independent step-child, central banking.

This theory of endogenous money is unique to Mises and his followers. No other school of economic opinion accepts it.

Every other school appeals to the State, as an exogenous coercive power, to regulate the money supply and create enough new fiat or credit money to keep the free market operational at nearly full employment with nearly stable prices. Every other theory of money invokes the use of the State's monopolistic power to supply the optimum quantity of money. No matter how often some non-Austrian School economist says that he is in favor of the free market, when it comes to his theory of money, he always says, "I believe in the free market, but. . . ." As Leonard Read wrote in 1970, we are sinking in a sea of buts.

When they are not outright collectivists, non-Austrian School economists are defenders of the so-called mixed economy: economic direction to the free market provided by State officials, on pain of punishment. This position is clearest in their universal promotion of non-market, State-regulated, central-bank money. Mises denied that there can be a mixed economy. There are only State directives that affect market operations, in most cases negatively. (Rothbard substituted, "in all cases negatively.")

Mises's theory of money offers hope. The public is in charge, not central bankers. The public will decide what money it prefers and how it will be used. The free market is economically sovereign, not the State. Monetary reform, when it comes, will be imposed from the bottom up.

If what he wrote is true, then we need not waste our time by building reformist sand castles in the air by designing sophisticated, top-down monetary reforms that voters do not understand, politicians do not have time to consider, and central bankers will successfully thwart for not being in their personal self-interest. The free market will triumph without the implementation of our well-intentioned but politically amateurish monetary reform schemes. Mises's theory of money and credit shows us why the central bankers cannot win, just as his theory of economic calculation showed us why Marxist central planners could not win. Unfortunately, it took seven decades of economic losses and about a hundred million needless deaths to confirm his theory.

Here is my advice: do not adopt a theory of money and banking until you understand the free market. Money and banking are not independent of the free market. They are extensions of the free market. When searching for a consistent theory of money, begin with a consistent theory of the free market. Begin here: *Human Action*, Chapter 15: "The Market," Part 1, "The Characteristics of the Market Economy."

> The market economy is the social system of the division of labor under private ownership of the means of production. Everybody acts on his own behalf; but everybody's actions aim at the satisfaction of other people's needs as well as at the satisfaction of his own. Everybody in acting serves his fellow citizens. Everybody, on the other hand, is served by his fellow citizens. Everybody is both a means and an end in himself, an ultimate end for himself and a means to other people in their endeavors to attain their own ends.
>
> This system is steered by the market. The market directs the individual's activities into those channels in which he best serves the wants of his fellow men. There is in the operation of the market no compulsion and coercion. The state, the social apparatus of coercion and compulsion, does not interfere with the market and with the citizens' activities directed by the market. It employs its power to beat people into submission solely for the prevention of actions destructive to the preservation and the smooth operation of the market economy. It protects the individual's life, health, and property against violent or fraudulent aggression on the part of domestic gangsters and external foes. Thus the state creates and preserves the environment in which the market economy can safely operate. The Marxian slogan "anarchic production" pertinently characterizes

this social structure as an economic system which is not directed by a dictator, a production tsar who assigns to each a task and compels him to obey this command. Each man is free; nobody is subject to a despot. Of his own accord the individual integrates himself into the cooperative system. The market directs him and reveals to him in what way he can best promote his own welfare as well as that of other people. The market is supreme. The market alone puts the whole social system in order and provides it with sense and meaning.

The market is not a place, a thing, or a collective entity. The market is a process, actuated by the interplay of the actions of the various individuals cooperating under the division of labor. The forces determining the—continually changing—state of the market are the value judgments of these individuals and their actions as directed by these value judgments. The state of the market at any instant is the price structure, i.e., the totality of the exchange ratios as established by the interaction of those eager to buy and those eager to sell. There is nothing inhuman or mystical with regard to the market. The market process is entirely a resultant of human actions. Every market phenomenon can be traced back to definite choices of the members of the market society.

The market process is the adjustment of the individual actions of the various members of the market society to the requirements of mutual cooperation. The market prices tell the producers what to produce, how to produce, and in what quantity. The market is the focal point to which the activities of the individuals converge. It is the center from which the activities of the individuals radiate.

The market economy must be strictly differentiated from the second thinkable—although not realizable—system of social cooperation under the division of labor; the system of social or governmental ownership of the means of production. This second system is commonly called socialism, communism, planned economy, or state capitalism. The market economy or capitalism, as it is usually called, and the socialist economy preclude one another. There is no mixture of the two systems possible or thinkable; there is no such thing as a mixed economy, a system that would be in part capitalist and in part socialist. Production is directed by the market or by the decrees of a production tsar or a committee of production tsars.

If within a society based on private ownership by the means of production some of these means are publicly owned and operated—that is, owned and operated by the government or one of its agencies—this does not make for a mixed system which would combine socialism and capitalism. The fact that the state or municipalities own and operate some plants does not alter the characteristic features of the market economy. The publicly owned and operated enterprises are subject to the sovereignty of the market. They must fit themselves, as buyers of raw materials, equipment, and labor, and as sellers of goods and services, into the scheme of the market economy. They are subject to the laws of the market and thereby depend on the consumers who may or may not patronize them. They must strive for profits or, at least, to avoid losses. The government may cover losses of its plants or shops by drawing on public funds. But this neither eliminates nor mitigates the supremacy of the market; it merely shifts it to another sector (pp. 258–59).

Index

action, 18
  as exchange, 18
America's Great Depression (Rothbard), 111
Austrian School of economics, 10, 32, 97, 127
Austrian Theory of the Trade Cycle and Other Essays, The (Mises), 114–15

Bank for International Settlements, 126
banking, 69–95
  cartels, 86–87, 93
  free banking, 85–87, 95
  functions of, 80–81
bankruptcy, 87, 110
barter, 13 *see also* direct exchange
Böhm-Bawerk, Eugen, 32
boom-bust business cycle, 78, 83–84, 95, 97, 106–109, 113–16
Bretton Woods agreement, 89, 124

Callahan, Gene, 11
capital goods, 31–32, 79
cash balances, 58–59
Causes of the Economic Crisis: An Address, The (Mises), 97
central bank, 84–93, 113, 115, 130–34
  final goal of, 88
Charles V (Spain), 70
circulation credit theory, 97
clearing price, 60
coin value, 21–23
  free coinage, 22–23, 26, 28
Coke, Sir Edward, 124
commodity money, 19–20, 26–27, 88
consumer credit, 107–108
consumption goods, 33, 81–82, 101–109
contracts, 71, 84, 87
  State enforcement of, 48, 50–51, 84, 86, 95, 113, 117, 119, 134
  violations of, 71–72
Counter-Revolution of Science, The (Hayek), 35
credit clearing-house systems, 44
credit expansion, 89
  see also inflation
credit money, 20, 21, 26–28, 69, 71–72, 83, 88, 92
  see also fractional reserve banking, fiduciary media
credit transactions, 15, 76–77

debasement of currency, 9, 71–72
  see also monetary debasement
Deep Throat, 78
depression see economic depression
direct exchange, 13
  see also barter
deflation, 41, 56 –57, 59, 61, 118–123, 130
  see also inflation
devaluation, 72
discount of future goods, 99–100
  see also interest rate

"Economic Calculation in the Socialist Commonwealth" (Mises), 7
economic depression, 98, 112
economic recession, 98, 114
Economics (Samuelson), 8
endogenous entrepreneurial market process, 60, 117, 134
Essays in Persuasion (Keynes), 50
Essay on the Nature and Significance of Economic Science, An (Robbins), 35

Federal Deposit Insurance Corporation (FDIC), 74, 105, 113
federal funds rate, 74
Federal Reserve Bank of New York, 125
Federal Reserve System, 87, 111, 122, 126
Fertig, Lawrence, 8
fiat money, 19–20, 27–28, 87, 88
fiduciary media, 21, 69–70, 78, 80–82, 85–89, 94, 105, 108–11, 118
  see also credit money, fractional reserve banking
first-order goods, see consumption goods
Fisher, Irving, 63
flexible money, 130
Foundation for Economic Education, 133
fractional reserve banking, 10, 36, 65, 69–95, 107, 113–15
  with a gold standard, 69–73
  without gold, 73–75
free market, 9, 28, 134–38

Genoa Accords, 89
gold demonetization, 72–73, 90, 125–126
gold-exchange standard, 89–93, 124
gold re-monetization, 127–30
gold standard, 10, 42–44, 46, 48–50, 64–65, 69, 71, 73, 79–80, 90–93, 119–25, 132–33
  international, 49, 65, 89
goldsmith banking, 69–70
Greenspan, 130–31
Gresham's law, 25–28, 128
Gresham, Sir Thomas, 25

Hayek, F. A., 9
Heilbroner, Robert, 8
higher-order goods, 103
Human Action: A Treatise on Economics (Mises), 8, 9, 16, 18, 20–22, 35, 36, 40–41, 46, 48, 53–54, 56, 58, 63, 65, 85, 89, 93, 95, 99–101, 107, 111–12, 124, 136–138

index numbers, 62–63, 67
indirect exchange, 13–14, 53
  see also money
inflation, 34–41, 45, 48, 75, 83–86, 95, 104, 130
  definition, 55–57
interest, 101

interest rate, 99–106
as a discount of future goods against present goods, 99–101
inflation premium, 100
market rate of interest, 102–103
originary (natural), 99–101, 108–110, 114
risk premium, 100, 110
International Monetary Fund, 88, 89
It's a Wonderful Life, 71

James I, King, 124

Keynes, John Maynard, 50
Knight, Frank H., 100

Liberalismus (Mises), 50–51
loans, 75–76, 80–81, 103

malinvestment, 111
Man, Economy, and State (Rothbard), 93
marginal utility, 38, 57
Menger, Carl, 16, 34
mining, 95
Mises, Ludwig von
theory of money, 13–28
see also nominalist theory of money
theory of the business cycle, *see* monetary theory of the business cycle
Mises Seminar, 8
mixed economy, 135, 138
monetary debasement, 9
monetary policy, 47–48, 117
freeze on money supply, 51, 117–20
monetary reform, 125–135
Monetary Stabilization and Cyclical Policy (Mises), 65
monetary theory of the business cycle, 83, 97–111, 113
money, 9
as a capital good, 31–32
definition of, 9, 14, 15, 22, 28, 31
function of, 13–15
kinds of, 19–28
measure of price, 19
medium of exchange, 13–15, 26
money-certificate, 20–21, 28, 48, 70
necessity of, 13
neutral money, 10, 53–54, 65, 67, 105, 116
new money, 37–40, 53
uneven spread of, 45–46, 57
optimum quantity of, 9, 31–46
purchasing power, 27
stable prices, 10, 43, 51, 53–54, 57–58, 61–66
State-issued, 42–43, 46
see also gold standard
State monopoly over, 29
supply of, 34–37
increase/decrease in, 34–41, 45–46, 80–83, 118
distribution of wealth, 41
transmission of value vs. measure of value, 16–19
value of, 32–33, 42, 44
Montaigne dogma, 40–41
Myrdal, Gunnar, 9

New Yorker, The, 8
Nobel Prize, 9
nominalist theory of money, 22–23
North, Gary, 10

objective theory of value, 18 , 47
see also subjective theory of value

Omnipotent Government (Mises), 132

Petition of Right, 124
Pogo Possum, 112
polylogism, 49
price, 56
  as exchange ratios, 28
  competition, 59, 61, 67
  control, 26–28
  government price-setting, 25
  Laws of, 24
production goods, 33, 101, 106–09
  goal of, 59–60
profit, 101
public welfare, 47, 54
purchasing power, 63–64

Read, Leonard E., 133, 135
recession *see* economic recession
redistribution of wealth, 46–47, 53, 67, 78–83, 95
Reed, Donna, 71
Robbins, Lionel, 9, 35
Rockwell, Llewellyn, 10
Roosevelt, Franklin, 72–73
Röpke, Wilhelm, 9
Rothbard, Murray, 47, 93, 111, 135

sacrifice, 76–77
Samuelson, Paul, 8
scarcity, 60–61
second-order goods *see* production goods
Sloan, Alfred, 107
social value, 34–36, 40–41, 51
Socialism: An Economic and Sociological Analysis (Mises), 7, 9
Solomon, 18
stable prices, 16 *see also* money
Stewart, Jimmy, 71
subjective theory of value, 16–19, 34–36, 41–42, 44, 47
  see also objective theory of value
  comparison of values, 18–19
  scales of value, 17–18, 35
subjective utility, 34–36

Theory of Money and Credit, The (Mises), 7, 9, 13–29, 31–35, 37–39, 42–45, 48, 54–56, 58, 61–64, 66, 71–72, 76–94, 100, 105–106, 119–21, 130
theory of the business cycle, 9, 10
time preference, 99, 114, 116
token coins, 20, 24–28

value, 16–19
  see also subjective/objective theory of value
  acts of valuation, 19
  laws of, 24
voluntary exchange, 13

Wanniski, Jude, 10
Watergate, 78
World Bank, 88
Woodward, Bob, 78

Made in the USA
Columbia, SC
19 June 2021

40387808R00080